KOBE

KOBE

LIFE LESSONS
FROM A LEGEND

NELSON PEÑA

CASTLE POINT BOOKS

NEW YORK

For Jenny
and all my heroes,
especially Julia, Valerie,
Peter, and Haydée Peña
—N.P.

www.castlepointbooks.com

The Castle Point Books trademark is owned by Castle Point
Publishing, LLC.
Castle Point books are published and distributed by St. Martin's
Publishing Group.

Design by Katie Jennings Campbell
Illustrations by Gilang Bogy

ISBN 978-1-250-27534-9 (paper over board)
ISBN 978-1-250-27535-6 (ebook)

Our books may be purchased in bulk for promotional,
educational, or business use. Please contact your local
bookseller or the Macmillan Corporate and Premium
Sales Department at 1-800-221-7945, extension 5442,
or by email at MacmillanSpecialMarkets@macmillan.com.

First Edition: 2021

10 9 8 7 6 5 4 3 2 1

"THE MOST IMPORTANT THING IS TO TRY AND INSPIRE PEOPLE SO THAT THEY CAN BE GREAT IN WHATEVER THEY WANT TO DO."

CONTENTS

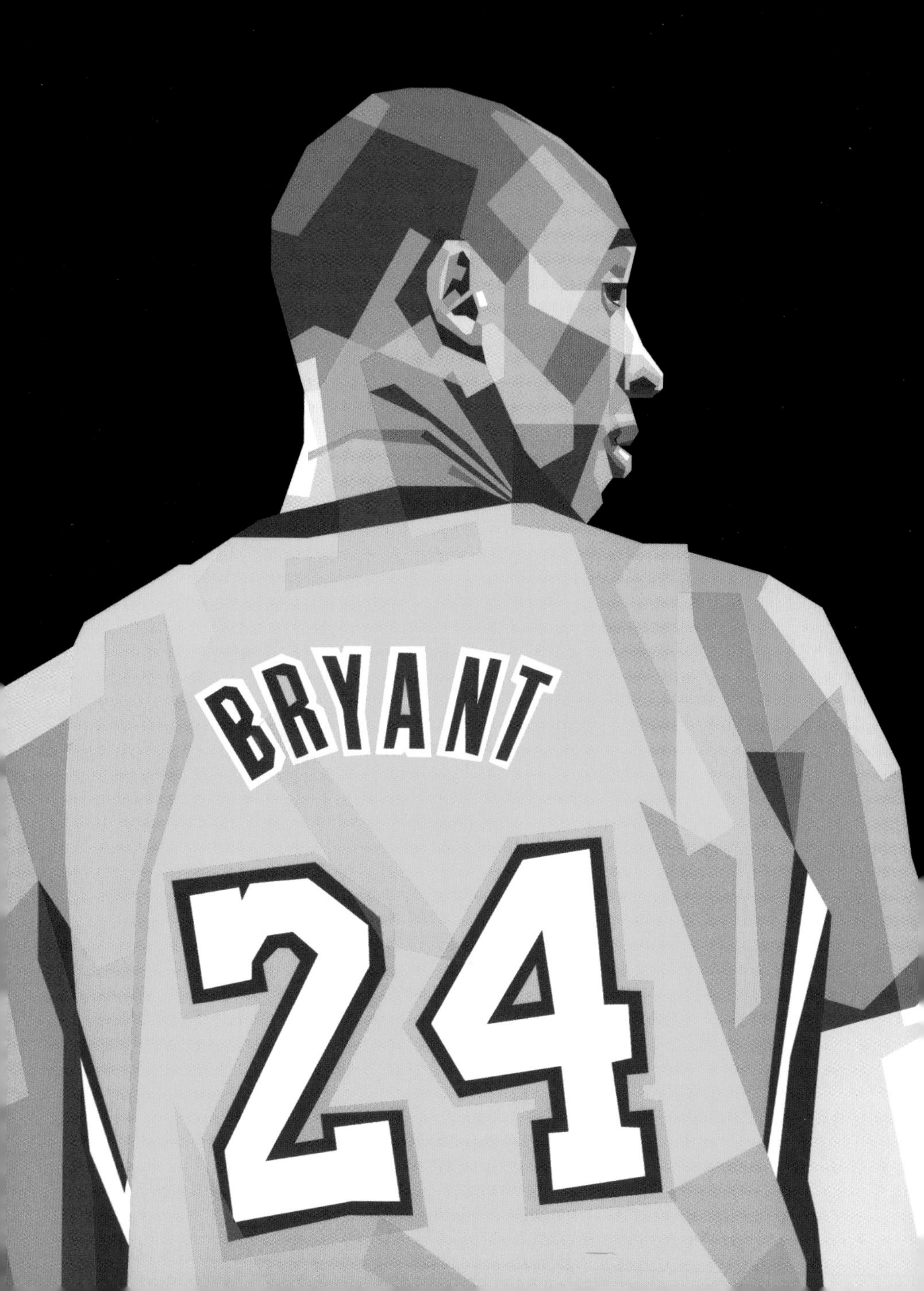
BRYANT
24

INTRODUCTION

Kobe Bryant loved to score. As every hoop fan knows, he once famously put up 81 points in a single game. Later, in his last appearance as a pro—the kind of moment when other past-their-prime athletes hope to just play respectably, take a bow, and wave a grateful good-bye to the crowd—Kobe had other ideas. He scored 60 points. In more than 20,000 NBA games played this century, featuring more than 200,000 starting players, only seven other players have scored 60 points in a game, and none more than once. When Kobe reached 60 in that final, unforgettable game, it was the sixth time he had done it.

More than scoring, though, Kobe loved winning. His high school squad won a state championship. With his next team, the Los Angeles Lakers, he won five NBA championships. Representing his country as part of the U.S. men's basketball team in 2008 and 2012, he won two Olympic gold medals. Overall, he was among the most decorated and successful players in basketball history, a Most Valuable Player and 18-time all-star selection, winning the NBA All-Star Game MVP so often that the league named the award after him.

The truth is, there was something that Kobe loved even more than scoring and winning. Beyond anything else, he loved working toward his goals. For Kobe Bryant, the secret to life was finding something you love and working as hard as possible to become the best at it. That's the approach he recommended to anyone who asked: Set big, audacious goals and blissfully lose yourself in the journey to get there. Kobe chased greatness.

To reach it, he tenaciously and passionately pursued his own self-improvement, and in the process found joy and purpose:

"The mindset isn't about seeking a result—it's more about the process of getting to that result. It's about the journey and the approach. It's a way of life. I do think that it's important, in all endeavors, to have that mentality."

Kobe was a rare and epic blend of intensity, wits, and grace. On the basketball court, he sometimes looked like the perfect player. He was smart and skilled; lean and athletic; fast and aggressive. But he wasn't perfect—far from it. There's much to learn from Kobe Bryant, but perfection is an illusion, and his story is more real than that. He faced serious struggles, on and off the court. He made major life-altering mistakes that hurt others. Like most people, he failed often. His is a tale of love and passion; perseverance and redemption; and the deep commitment that gives life meaning.

"I LEARNED TO FOCUS ON THE TASK AT HAND, ON THE PREPARATION, ON THE BATTLE."

He was a baller. He considered the game his craft and devoted most of his years to reaching its highest level through relentless planning, physical work, mental training, tenacity, and a commitment to continued learning. He developed habits and philosophies that anyone can apply to their life. He paid attention to details and fell in love with the pursuit of excellence. Later he used the same principles that made him a pro athlete on a different quest, a creative one: He was determined to become a legendary storyteller on the level of Walt Disney or J. K. Rowling. He was off to a strong start, winning an Oscar for one of his first efforts, before his life was cut short by a helicopter crash at the age of 41.

Kobe wanted to set a good example and leave a lasting legacy. He didn't always live up to that ambition. But he spent most of his life trying and, ultimately, succeeding. For millions, he was an inspiration—exhilarating and unforgettable. There was power in his unfiltered passion and dedication, and something extraordinary about his raw intensity—the way he seemed so certain of his dreams, and so determined to make them real. He believed in paying it forward and spent a lot of time helping others benefit from his experience and approach. Even now, after his passing, his best lessons continue to inspire and teach. All we have to do is look closely at his life to see the crucial ingredients that made him a legend.

FIND WHAT YOU LOVE

Kobe found his love early. His father, Joe "Jellybean" Bryant, played in the NBA for eight years. Then Joe signed with an Italian team and moved the family to the small, ancient town of Rieti when Kobe was six. For the next seven years, as Joe bounced from one Italian team to another, his son felt like the outsider—a Black American kid dropped into Italian culture:

"I grew up in isolation," said Kobe. "It was not an environment suited to me. I was the only Black kid. I didn't speak the language. I'd be in one city, but then we'd move to a different city and I'd have to do everything again." He learned to be on his own in those years, because he didn't have much of a choice. He came to see that trying to fit in wasn't worth the effort: "I'd make friends but I'd never be part of the group, because the other kids were already growing up together." He learned to speak Italian fluently, but still saw himself as a loner. He tried soccer, where his size made him a natural goalie, but basketball was an even better escape. The more he played, the more he realized that he had discovered something special; something to ease the frustration of feeling overlooked. Something that would create a space just for him:

> *"I had all this anger inside of me that I hadn't really let out. No matter what happened in life, I could always step on to the court and just absolutely erupt. The feeling of playing with that rage was new to me, but I [expletive] loved it. Once I discovered that, everything about the game changed."*

When his parents bought him an official leather NBA basketball, he slept with it. He would go to bed in his basketball clothes so that he would be ready in case his dad asked him to tag along for morning practice with the pro team. Joe often brought his son to practice after school, too. Kobe's grandfather sent videotapes of American basketball games, and the young player couldn't get enough of them. He showed a curiosity for how the game was played that was unusual for someone of his age. Instead of just collecting basketball cards like his friends, he would study the photos to figure out exactly what moves the players were executing and, as he explained it, "which of their muscles were firing to make the move happen." He'd then go about developing those muscles and moves for himself.

WORK IT

He played on local teams in Italy where he got the benefit of a strong hoops education. While American basketball valued strength and athleticism, European coaches were known for drilling the fundamentals of the game, with a

"IT WAS BASKETBALL ALL DAY."

particular focus on proper footwork and shooting, two skill sets that would later serve him well. He worked hard and caught on quickly, and it already showed. When he was about 11 years old, an Italian professional team inquired about

made an impression on him. "I'm not talking like, you know, shagging rebounds, like a ball boy or whatever," Shaw said. "I'm talking, this kid was in the layup line like he was on the team. He was out there shooting Js with the players."

SEARCHING FOR AN EDGE

Over his career, Kobe's deals with shoe companies produced 22 signature sneakers. While the shoe companies viewed their partnerships as a way to promote products, Kobe saw them as something else: a chance to gain an advantage. He had Nike add a special alloy band inside the arch to cut a fraction of a second off his reaction time. He also asked Nike to design a shoe with a sock already attached inside the shoe. His theory was that when he made a move on the basketball court, his foot would slide—ever so slightly—inside his shoe, slowing him down. If the sock and shoe were attached, there would be less slide, and more speed.

buying his future rights, an idea that his parents nixed.

That same year, NBA player Brian Shaw was playing in Italy and encountered him for the first time. Shaw remembers a game against Joe Bryant's team in Rome with young Kobe hanging around the pros as they warmed up. Kobe

At one point, Shaw asked the preteen kid to please get out of the way, and Kobe, never bashful, challenged him to a game of H-O-R-S-E. Shaw, who was 22 at the time and already had a year of NBA experience, figures that he probably let the kid win, but now has no clear memory of who prevailed. Kobe remembered; after a long NBA playing career, Shaw later became an assistant coach with the Lakers, and together again after all those years, Kobe often teased Shaw about how he beat him when he was just 11.

When Kobe was 13, the Bryants moved back to the U.S. and settled into a comfortable, 3,400-square-foot colonial style home near Philadelphia. Once again, he was the outsider who didn't quite fit into any specific category—this time as the "rich" Black kid from Italy standing out in a white neighborhood. To escape and find some joy, he turned to the thing he loved most, the sport that made him want to work to be his best. He led Lower Merion High School to its first boys' basketball state title in 53 years, posting a 73-14 record in his last three seasons. Addicted to the game, Kobe practiced by himself at five in the morning and sometimes late into the night. By the time he was a senior, he was a McDonald's All-American and had been named the Naismith High School Player of the Year and Gatorade Men's National Basketball

Player of the Year. That spring of 1996, at age 17, when Kobe took the unusual step of entering the NBA draft directly from high school, he was finally able to give his first love his undivided attention:

"The thing I was most excited about was coming to the NBA not having to . . . worry about writing a paper or doing homework."

The kid who always loved hoops above all else had found his bliss.

SWEAT THE DETAILS
In the world of Kobe Bryant, no detail was too small. Every edge, even a tiny one, was worth gaining. This was his definition of being a professional NBA competitor. He iced the back of his knees, not just the front. He even studied the referee's handbook and absorbed nuances to help his game. As a play begins, each ref has an area of the court that they're responsible for, and those locations move as the ball moves. "When they do that," Kobe explained, "it creates dead zones, areas on the court where they

"IF YOU LOVE THE GAME, THEN YOU'VE ALREADY WON."

can't see certain things. I learned where those zones were, and I took advantage of them. I would get away with holds, travels and all sorts of minor violations because I took the time to understand the officials' limitations."

Before the start of his fourth NBA season, an errant elbow fractured a bone in his right hand, causing him to miss 15 games. After he returned to action, he noticed his free-throw percentage dipping slightly. This wasn't really a cause for alarm—his 82 percent shooting was among the Top 35 in the league. But by studying video footage, he realized that the way his fingers were taped for protection had inadvertently changed his grip. His four fingers weren't evenly spaced on the ball anymore, and his shots were rotating slightly to the right. It was a fairly minor thing, but he

committed to fixing the issue. Over the course of the next summer, he worked on it, focusing on his grip and making 100,000 shots. In telling the story, he always emphasized that this was 100,000 shots *made*, not *taken*. He explained that he never practiced *taking* shots, he practiced *making* them. And most weren't easy. Over and over, he rehearsed the kind of dynamic and difficult shots that he took in games. The following season, he raised his scoring average from an impressive 22.5 points per game to a star-level 28.5. His free-throw percentage rose to 85 percent, putting him in the Top 20 in the league. Nobody would have noticed the finger-spacing adjustment he made, but Kobe knew it had made a difference.

DECLARE YOUR LOVE

When the time comes to announce their retirement, most star athletes call a press conference or post a message on their social media. Not Kobe Bryant. In 2015, at the age of 37, as he began his record 20th and final season with the same NBA team, Kobe signaled his departure with a love poem.

He addressed it to his beloved, the one that had inspired and intrigued him for 35 years. He called his poem "Dear Basketball," and in it, he laid bare his obsessive passion for the game. This poem would eventually be transformed by Kobe's company, Granity Studios, into an animated short film, later deemed the best of the year by the Academy of Motion Picture Arts and Sciences. In it, we see Kobe as an animated toddler shooting his dad's rolled-up socks into a garbage can, imagining that they are game-winning shots for the Lakers. Kobe narrates:

"I fell in love with you.
A love so deep I gave you my all—
From my mind & body
To my spirit & soul."

He continues:

"I did everything for YOU
Because that's what you do
When someone makes you feel as
Alive as you've made me feel."

"IF YOU REALLY WANT TO BE GREAT AT SOMETHING, YOU HAVE TO TRULY CARE ABOUT IT. YOU HAVE TO OBSESS OVER IT."

"THE BEAUTY IN BEING BLESSED WITH TALENT IS RISING ABOVE DOUBTERS TO CREATE A BEAUTIFUL MOMENT."

For Kobe, the poem was a fitting farewell to his beloved sport. He was an athlete renowned for his tenacity and aggressiveness. But at his core, that intensity was grounded in a more tender emotion. It was pure love.

If we are lucky, at some point in our lives we find something as important to us as basketball was to Kobe Bryant. He was crazy about it—so crazy that he dreamed he could be the greatest player ever and spent decades consumed by the pursuit. Every pro athlete works hard to get where they are, but nobody worked harder than him,

and it's unlikely anyone ever loved basketball more.

You could see this best in the quiet moments, away from the spotlight. In Los Angeles, the Drew League is a no-frills summer league where good basketball players test themselves against other good players. Some are pros. Most aren't. In 2011, Kobe and a young James Harden both showed up on the same day and had a showdown that observers still recall with awe, each scoring more than 40 points before Kobe made the game-winning shot. As his shot dropped, he kept his arms held high in victory and was swarmed by the

"I DON'T PLAY FOR THE FAME."

small crowd. There were no TV cameras or awards. But he couldn't have cared less. This was what Kobe cherished most. The game. The battle. The squeaks of sneakers on hardwood. A shirt so drenched in sweat that he had to wring it out. The thrill of trying and triumph.

DO IT FOR YOURSELF— NO ONE ELSE

Like anyone in love with what they do, Kobe was obsessed. "I had a constant craving, a yearning, to improve and be the best," he wrote in his book, *The Mamba Mentality*. Even in a profession filled with big egos and alpha dogs, his intensity and tenacity stood out. His insatiable desire for the game was the source of his power. He couldn't think of himself as separate from the sport he played.

Kobe's work ethic was well rewarded. In addition to the championships, MVP awards, and the Oscar, there were large paychecks. By the time he left basketball, he had made $680 million in salary and endorsements in his NBA playing career, the highest total for any team-sport athlete in history, according to *Forbes*. No doubt the money and the lifestyle it brought were sweet, as were the adulation and deep esteem he earned from his profession. Young players

---

STAT ⚡ Kobe was the first guard to skip college basketball and enter the NBA draft straight out of high school.

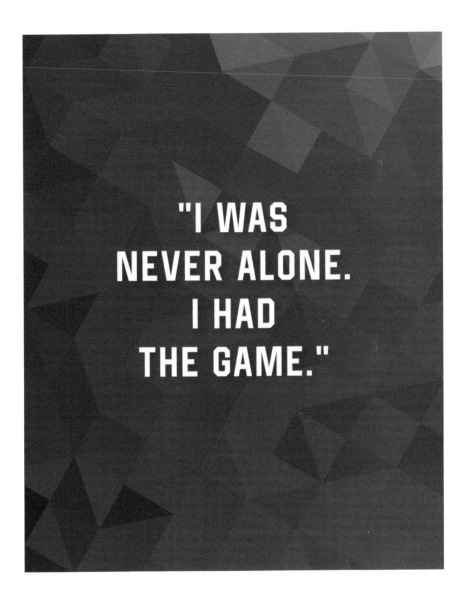

"I WAS
NEVER ALONE.
I HAD
THE GAME."

worshipped him and will for many years to come. When he retired, generations of older players, including many of the all-time greats, expressed their high regard.

He appreciated the kind words. When an ESPN reporter asked him about the accolades he'd received from players past, Kobe responded, "That's awesome because that means that these guys, who were my muses growing up, respect the way that I've carried on their legacy." But he also made something else clear: He didn't define himself by their words or their approval. "What is validation, really?" he asked. "What does it do for you? That does not complete me as a man or make me feel fulfilled."

Those who knew him well say that while the money and admiration were appreciated, his true motivation was always more internal. He worked hard—not for the rewards, but because he loved it.

PIVOT WITH PURPOSE
When Kobe was nearing retirement, he rejected the idea of being a

"I LOVE BASKETBALL SO MUCH. I HAVE SO MUCH FIRE. IT'S PART OF ME, MAN. IT'S LIKE HEAVEN."

coach, team owner, or basketball broadcaster. While he respected those roles, he knew nothing in basketball could fulfill him the way playing did. He needed to be all-in or all-out. He didn't want a life on the margins. But he worried about the struggle to find something meaningful. "I'll be damned if I retire without a purpose," he insisted. "That's not going to happen to me." So, he moved on, and devoted himself to a new love, becoming a master storyteller and working to build a media enterprise for the ages.

He had previously put together a small company with no real mission, just the vague goal of earning as much money as possible. He later considered this directionless approach a huge mistake. To succeed, he knew he needed passion. As part of a brainstorming technique to point him in a new direction, he was asked to list the most fun things he had ever done outside of basketball. He recalled a high school English assignment where he was asked to tell an original story to a class of kindergartners. Kobe's tale was about a kid who never cleaned his room. He depicted a scene where the objects the main character left out came to life and transformed into monsters, scaring the kid enough that he never had a messy room again. Kobe recalled how much his young audience loved the story, and how it had actually persuaded some of the listeners to clean their rooms. Kobe reveled in the memory. He thought of the impact he had made long ago and considered the power of storytelling. It was a tool he could use to teach others.

He had his new storytelling vision and, from the start, he approached it Kobe-style, focusing intensely on the small stuff. He began watching his favorite movies five times each, his focus shifting with each viewing. First, he'd watch it as a fan, then he'd view it again concentrating on the director's decisions, then again focused on the lighting, then the music, then he'd watch it with the sound off to absorb the visuals one more time. When he got together with friends, he would consult their kids

"I COULD TELL THAT THE GAME MEANT MORE TO ME THAN TO EVERYBODY ELSE."

like they were a mini focus group, bouncing show concepts off them.

Throughout all of Kobe's creative ventures, he was decidedly hands-on. In 2017, as part of a six-video deal he struck with ESPN, he produced a puppet show. When he didn't like the texture of the puppet snake, he had the designers change it. Similarly, after a table read for another ESPN show he was developing, he approached the actors and implored them to practice together at least two hours a day. He wanted everyone to be as fully engaged as he was. For someone as dedicated as Kobe, it was crucial to be surrounded by like-minded people. When he was

able to control who he worked with, he only considered people who were "all-in," who he admiringly referred to as "obsessives." No one else needed to apply.

He would rather work alone than work with people who didn't give it everything they had. On the basketball court, he couldn't work in isolation, but he often felt isolated. Kobe knew that his commitment to his work made him different. "Other guys could leave it afterward and detach from it. I couldn't. It stuck with me. I thought about it all night." Throughout his life, he would head to the gym at all hours (even at three or four a.m.) to work on his game and to "smell the scent" of the place. This passionate dedication fueled everything. Kobe explained it like this:

"Some of these guys don't love the game. . . . It's a job for them. And when something is a job, you can have success for a week, two weeks, a month, maybe a year, maybe even two. Then you'll fall. It's inevitable. But if you love it, you can't be stopped."

During his playing days, Kobe was seen as a loner, content to develop his game rather than hang out with his teammates. Obsessed and enamored with his craft, he often isolated himself to work on skills, and in the process, made few close friends. But this single-minded approach was at the heart of his success, and he wouldn't have had it any other way. After all, this was love.

LESSONS FROM A LEGEND

- **DISCOVER WHAT YOU LOVE THE MOST AND COMMIT TO IT FULLY.**
- **FOCUS ON THE LITTLE THINGS. NO DETAIL IS TOO SMALL.**
- **DON'T PRACTICE TAKING SHOTS. PRACTICE *MAKING* SHOTS.**
- **SURROUND YOURSELF WITH DEDICATED PEOPLE.**

SEE THE BIG PICTURE

Kobe was known for striking with lightning quickness on the court. In a pressure situation, he was famous for his ability to rise up and meet the moment. But there was another aspect to him that got less attention: He was a meticulous planner. When he achieved a moment of glory, it wasn't by chance or even just by talent. He had long ago dreamed it, envisioned it, prepared for it, and took specific action to be ready for the opportunity—often many months or years in advance.

In January 2006, he recorded his famed 81-point game, one of the greatest individual performances in sports history. This was a pinnacle moment in his life, but it didn't just happen. He had long visualized himself scoring 80 or 90 points in a game, planned for it, then took the necessary steps to get there. Afterward, he looked back and knew exactly how he did it: "I had worked extremely hard the summer before that," he said, referring to his epic game. "[It] was a culmination of days and days of hard work."

"PEOPLE DON'T REMEMBER THE PEOPLE WHO COME IN SECOND."

Setting a long-range goal and going after it was how Kobe lived his life. It was a very grown-up habit that he exhibited even as a kid. He would shoot baskets during halftime at his dad's pro games in Italy, and his performance was so good that he drew a big reaction in the arena. Playing the star in a professional setting would be enough to launch NBA dreams for any kid. Kobe, though, backed up the dream with a solid and precise plan that set him on a path to his own pro career.

When he moved back to the U.S., Kobe read a basketball magazine that ranked him as the 57th best prospect in his 13-year-old age group. He started sizing up the competition. "At 13 years old I had a kill list," he said. He began focusing on all the players ranked in front of him. He started with No. 56, then No. 55, and then every player up to the kid ranked No. 1. When he got to each player, he researched which AAU youth circuit team they played for, and when they met on the court, he studied them: "That became my mission in high school: to check off every other person, all those 56 other names, hunt them down, and knock them down."

"Knocking them down" didn't mean beating his rivals or even being the most impressive player on the court on any given day. He had bigger plans. An AAU game was just a skirmish. Kobe wanted to win the war. He wanted to be the best in a few years when colleges came recruiting. Kobe explained his approach to watching his young opponents:

> *"I would size you up and see what your strengths and weaknesses are. How do you approach the game? Are you silly about it? Are you goofy about it? Are you good at it just because you're bigger and stronger than everybody else? Or is there actually thought and skill that you put into it?*
>
> *At 13 years old, I played the longer game because my game wasn't about being better than you at 13. It was to be better than you when the chips were really on the line."*

As part of his meticulous approach, he put himself through the same intense analysis, and came to realize his own weaknesses. But the AAU summer schedule was jammed with games, and there wasn't much time to practice skills and improve. Desperate to stand out, his rivals would use the games to show off their talents and pile up victories. "When you're playing in competition," he explained, "you're only playing to your strengths. Why? Because you want to win." Kobe saw the weakness in that approach over the long haul and took a different tack:

> *"I played to my weaknesses. I wouldn't play to my strengths. I would work on the things in those games that I was weak at—left hand, pull-up jump shot, my postgame. I had a strategy. So then fast forward to when I'm 17 and my game is completely well rounded—and that player I saw at 13 is still doing the same [expletive] at 17. Now you got a problem."*

His plan took a few years to kick in, but it worked. No. 57 became No. 1.

SET YOUR SIGHTS HIGH

Kobe always had the ability to take a broad view. Growing up in two countries speaking multiple languages, he developed a wide, unlimited perspective of what was possible. In March 1996, when he was a senior in high school, he met two of the most transcendent basketball players of all time in a corridor after an NBA game at the old Philadelphia Spectrum. Joe Bryant had arranged for his son to have a few moments with Michael Jordan and Julius Erving. Thrust into a conversation with these hoop gods, most teenagers would be starstruck and a bit shy. Kobe had no such problem.

At the time, the idea of high school players jumping directly to the NBA was almost unheard of. But cocky and goal-oriented Kobe declared to his heroes that he was ready to enter the NBA draft that June. Jordan and Erving made brief eye contact with each other and shared a knowing glance, smiling at the youthful brashness, but also recognizing a kindred spirit. "I was

"IT'S NOT DONE IN ONE SUMMER. IT'S ABOUT HAVING A FIVE-YEAR PLAN, A TEN-YEAR-PLAN, AND UNDERSTANDING HOW TO GET THERE."

a little psychopath," Kobe said, thinking back. "I was as obsessed as they were."

A month later, he announced his plan publicly. At a press conference in his high school gym, he said, "I've decided to skip college and take my talent to the NBA," (coining a phrase that would become part of hoop lore). But rather than sit back and wait to see which team would draft him, he and his advisors put in place a bold, unusual plan. His agent let the NBA know that the 17-year-old wanted to play for his hometown Philadelphia 76ers (who had the first pick in the draft) or for his favorite team, the Lakers (who would be choosing 24th), and that if he didn't get his wish he would go back to Europe and play there. It was a risky strategy, but it paid off. The teams at the top of the draft ignored him. The Charlotte Hornets, choosing 13th, swung a deal, arranging to choose him and immediately trade him to the Lakers. Through hard work, talent, planning, and nerve, the kid who had always imagined himself playing for the Lakers had made it happen.

NEVER BE SATISFIED

Central to the Kobe Bryant philosophy is that when a big goal is reached, you don't rest. Rather, that's when you set another substantial objective and get to work. It's OK if that objective might be far into the future. Driven by strong ambition and a big imagination, he was focused on more than just instant gratification. When he arrived in L.A., it was clear that the team would be led by Shaquille O'Neal, one of the game's most dominant players. Kobe craved a bigger role, and it didn't take long before he began forming a blueprint for his future. "I'm only 21," he pointed out, slyly. "When I'm 28, Shaq will be what, 40?" He was tweaking his teammate and brotherly rival, who was only six years his senior. But there was a truth hidden in his gibe. "Point is," he said with assuredness, "my time will come."

He kept more than one long-range goal in sight. He appeared solo on the cover of *Forbes* in an Armani suit, with the headline "The New Stars of Money" and the caption "Kobe Bryant shoots for a global market." He was not yet 22. That year, *Sports Illustrated* reported his plans for "Kobe Family Entertainment," a film production company to produce movies and sitcoms. These seeds grew to become the Oscar-winning studio that he launched 16 years later.

His secret was not just that he set big, audacious goals that motivated him to work hard. He also had an exceptional ability to stay true to those goals, and not get distracted by enticing new possibilities. When he retired, only two players had scored more points in NBA history: Kareem Abdul-Jabbar and Karl Malone. Asked late in his career if he wanted to stick around and chase the No. 1 spot, he had no interest. "If my goal had been going after Jabbar, I would have done that. I would have gone to a different team and scored 37 points a game. That was never my goal. My goal is to sit at the table with Michael and Magic, having won the same number of titles." In the end, Kobe got his seat at the mythic table, matching Magic Johnson's five NBA championships, just one short of Jordan.

MAKE DEEP SACRIFICES

Setting big goals is one thing; reaching them is the hard part, and for that he believed in sacrifice. He thought many of his competitors loved the game, but were not fully committed:

> *"Some people try to balance that love with other interests, but there's no such thing as balance. Either you want to be one of the greats, and you understand the sacrifices that come with it and deal with them, or you don't want to deal with them and you want to be in the middle of the pack."*

For Kobe, this was an article of faith: On the path to achievement, distractions are the enemy. Sacrifice was everything. His high school coach remembers him as a loner, with basketball taking the place

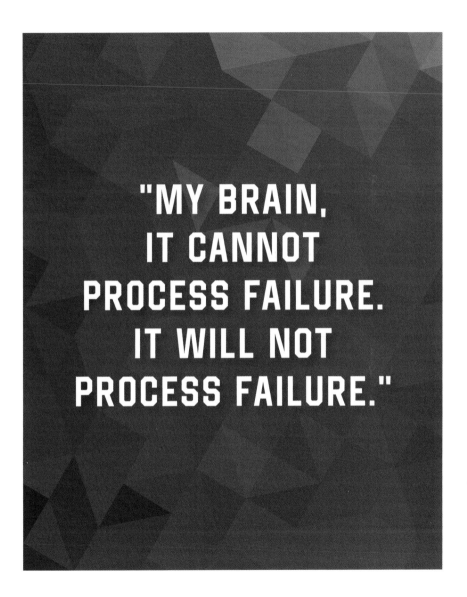

"MY BRAIN,
IT CANNOT
PROCESS FAILURE.
IT WILL NOT
PROCESS FAILURE."

of a social life. As a pro, even the bright lights of Hollywood didn't divert his drive. In his rookie year, he was offered the starring role in Spike Lee's *He Got Game,* the big basketball movie starring Denzel Washington. Filming was to begin after the season, but Kobe wanted to improve his skills and spend the off-season in the gym, so he turned down the iconic director.

IMMERSE YOURSELF

Kobe was annoyed by well-known players who publicly declared that they wanted to be great, but privately didn't put in the work. For many, the focus was enjoying the party life and fame. For others, it was family and other obligations of adulthood. Kobe was surprised that so many players took vacations at all. Satisfied with their enormous contracts, nobody seemed as hungry for success as Kobe expected:

> *"What I found in the NBA is a lot of guys played for financial stability. When they came to the NBA they got that financial stability, so therefore the passion and the work ethic and the obsessiveness was gone. So, I'm looking at that and I'm like, 'Oh my, this is going to be like taking candy from a baby.'"*

But it wasn't quite that easy. He underestimated the enormity of effort that his goals would require. "That [knowledge] isn't something I came into the league with. I don't think anybody does. You come in with the intent of playing hard, but you don't get the entire concept, how it operates, how it unfolds. That comes with time." Some players buckle under the challenge. Kobe held strong. If hard work was all he needed to be great, he knew he could do that, and he knew how: total immersion.

This type of long-range commitment limited time for friends or family. Even several seasons into his career, he said he had no friends on the team or anywhere in Los Angeles. At 21, he lived with his parents and older sister, and spent virtually all his time on basketball. By the time his career ended, he had made room

"IT BOTHERED ME WHEN SOMETHING FELT LIKE A WEAKNESS."

in his life for a loving wife and the daughters he adored, but outside of family, his professional dedication still crowded out deep friendships.

"I can be a *good* friend, but not a *great* friend," he said at age 36. "A great friend will call you every day and remember your birthday. I'll get so wrapped up in my [expletive], I'll never remember that stuff. The people who are my friends understand this, and they're usually the same way."

In fact, his best personal connections tended to be with people who also had an exceptionally strong work ethic. To others, he was exhausting. In practice, his intensity irritated some teammates. He understood why. "I am a maniacal worker," he admitted, "and if you're not working as hard as I am, I am going to let you know about it." As always, his eyes were on the prize.

WORK ON YOUR FLAWS

Shortcomings annoyed Kobe Bryant, especially his own. At age 6, it made him uneasy that he could only write with one hand, so he taught himself to use both. "I worked really hard on my left hand at that age. Specifically, I would brush my teeth with my left hand. I would write my name with my left hand. I hated the feeling of being uncomfortable." In high school and in the NBA, he brought the same self-improvement mindset to his game, working endlessly on weak points—midrange shooting,

> **"WHAT SEPARATES GREAT PLAYERS FROM ALL-TIME GREAT PLAYERS IS THEIR ABILITY TO SELF-ASSESS, DIAGNOSE WEAKNESSES, AND TURN THOSE FLAWS INTO STRENGTHS."**

3-point shooting, defense—until they were strengths.

Over time, he made his plans reality, and emerged as one of the most well-rounded players in NBA history with zero vulnerabilities in his skill set. "I build my game to have no holes," he declared. Other players marveled at his incredible volume of well-developed moves and countermoves. Most players have three or four. Kobe had 10. When he retired, he was lauded for developing the most complete arsenal of offensive weaponry that the game had ever seen.

What made Kobe so special was that he combined that firepower with an incredible sense of personal vision and clarity. He knew exactly what he wanted to do with his talent. He was proud of his father's long professional career, but he always wondered why his dad was a journeyman rather than a star. Kobe was clear on this fact: He wanted more. He was determined to battle his shortcomings in the name of success. In the end, he got it, of course. He not only won championships, he scored more points in some seasons than his dad had in his whole NBA career.

THINK LONG

Kobe took a far-sighted view of his athletic career, but his ability to think long didn't end with basketball. When he established Granity Studios, he talked about the next 50 years of possible achievements, and made a 20-year plan. It included a matrix of movies, podcasts, animation, television series, books, and more, with an intersecting collection of characters, fantasy lands, and stories. His associates were stunned by the vision. "It scares the hell out of them when we start talking about amusement parks," he noted, wryly.

The Granity concept came to him while flying home after practice during his final season and gazing out the window at all the little houses below. "If you look at all the potential stories—how the home is constructed, the family that lives there—there are infinite possibilities." But this was clearly no idle daydream. Inspired by complex popular sagas such as the *Lord of the Rings* and *Star Wars*, he could see a whole new world emerge. He knew he'd always be a famous former basketball player, but once his Granity plan got going, he believed the public would see him as

---

STAT ⚡ The prestigious All-NBA First Team honors the five best players in basketball every season. Michael Jordan was selected 10 times. Kobe, 11.

much more. He made a prediction: "When I go full bore into my second act, I think they will know me for something else."

The Kobe method—setting an objective, making a detailed plan, and doing the work to achieve it—gave him a single-minded, no-distractions lifestyle. It came with downsides, though, including that frustrating lack of close friends. He knew he had paid a price: "In terms of having one of those great, bonding friendships, that's something I will probably never have." It bothered him. He even went so far as to describe it as a "weakness." Ultimately, though, he accepted the sacrifices he made and was satisfied with his decisions. He found comfort and profound contentment with everything he envisioned and ultimately achieved in his long career. Just before he left basketball, Kobe coined and literally trademarked a phrase that he thought captured this feeling well: "Friends hang sometimes. Banners hang forever."

Having an eye on *forever* was typical Kobe Bryant. When he committed himself to something, it rarely was for a short-term payoff. After his playing career ended, in addition

"WE CAN ALL BE MASTERS AT OUR CRAFT, BUT YOU HAVE TO MAKE A CHOICE."

to focusing on building Granity, he began coaching his daughter Gianna and her young basketball teammates. As a coach, his interest went far beyond the scoreboard or season record. At one point, a reporter noted that Gianna's team of 12-year-olds still had much to improve. His remarkable response underscored his view of success as a long continuum—not just a moment. "You should have seen us six months ago. The girls are making incredible progress. Just wait until you see us in six years." Not six weeks or six months. Six years. It was the same approach Kobe had back in Italy when he was Gianna's age, eyes always focused far up the road.

LESSONS FROM A LEGEND

- **DREAM BIG. NEVER BE EMBARRASSED TO PUT YOUR AMBITIONS OUT THERE.**
- **MAKE SACRIFICES TO GET TO WHERE YOU WANT TO GO.**
- **DON'T HIT THE BRAKES WHEN YOU GET A LITTLE SUCCESS. HIT THE GAS.**
- **TURN WEAKNESSES INTO STRENGTHS.**

BE RELENTLESS

CHAPTER 3

When Kobe left basketball, his rivals breathed a sigh of relief and paid tribute to his incredible competitiveness. In interviews all over the hoop world, the words spoken were strikingly consistent. Killer. Assassin. Destroyer of dreams. One of his Olympic coaches, Jim Boeheim, who has been involved in basketball for nearly half a century, called him "the hardest working player I've ever been around." Doc Rivers, a longtime NBA coach who faced him in two championship series, openly celebrated his leaving, and spoke for many when he said, "I have great respect for him, but he inflicted a lot of pain on the rest of us."

This aggressive image was exactly what Kobe had always wanted. Unlike many sports stars who cultivate an affable, commercial-friendly persona away from the game and ham it up in burger and soda ads, Kobe represented a different vibe. He was serious and had only one gear: drive. His magazine covers almost always featured a scowl, not a smile. On the court, he was famous for a particularly menacing look that he would flash when at his most competitive—chin jutting out, lower teeth bared, eyes boring a hole through their target. For those trying to stop him, it was a look of determination not soon forgotten.

DO WHAT IT TAKES

Late in his career, the Lakers surrounded Kobe with a team of established veterans, including Steve Nash, Pau Gasol, Metta World Peace, and Dwight Howard. Expectations were high, but the mix didn't work and the team stumbled badly. Near the end of the season, it looked like this squad of stars might not even make the playoffs, an embarrassing result that Kobe had only suffered once in his first 16 years in the NBA. As things fell apart, he dug in. For the first time in his career, he publicly guaranteed that the Lakers would make the playoffs. He wanted to make it clear that he hadn't accepted defeat: "It had to be understood—we're doing this thing. It's not a wishy-washy thing. It's,

'No, we're *doing it.*'" When asked if that guarantee brought added pressure to him and his team, he replied, "Yeah, but I loved it. I [expletive] loved it. It pushed me to a level that I had never been to before—ever—in my career."

He had played extensive minutes all season and it took a toll on his body. A teammate told ESPN that Kobe was so worn down he could barely speak after games and seemed more like a 105-year-old woman than a 34-year-old NBA player. But now, with the playoffs on the line, he insisted on playing even more. In the last seven games he played that season, he averaged almost 46 minutes a game, a staggering total in a year when the minutes leader averaged less than 39. His coach, Mike D'Antoni, knew he needed rest, but found it impossible to get his stubborn superstar out of the game. "There was no denying him from doing what he wanted to do," D'Antoni said. "We tried."

Standing between Kobe Bryant and a goal was always a dangerous place

"I'M RELENTLESS. I WANT TO WIN. AND I WANT TO WIN BY ANY MEANS NECESSARY, AND THAT'S WHEN THE DEMON COMES OUT."

to be. The team trainer said even "if Jesus came down" and asked him to sit, the superstar guard wouldn't listen. D'Antoni felt like he had no choice: "I didn't think we should get into a wrestling match right there in front of 19,000 people, and that's what it would've taken to get him out of the game, and he just wouldn't come out. It was unbelievable." Kobe wanted to win so badly that he started taking over all aspects on the court. He took control and wouldn't relinquish it: "I called every play," he said. "I positioned everybody on the floor."

The Lakers needed to win almost every game in that stretch, and they did, with a weary Kobe averaging around 30 points, eight assists, seven rebounds, two steals, and one block per game. But ultimately, it seems he pushed his body too far. In the last weekend of the season, in the third quarter of a tight game, he drove to the basket and after crashing into a wall of defenders, found himself rolling on the court, grabbing his left knee in pain. He stayed in. A few minutes later, he landed awkwardly after a shot, and again the game stopped for a right-leg injury, as he grimaced and hobbled badly around the court. It didn't look like he could continue, but again he stayed in.

For the next quarter, he put mind over matter and dominated. It was classic Kobe, with his familiar spin moves and long threes keeping the Lakers close. Down two points in the final minutes, he drove to the basket, and feeling an intense shooting pain behind his left ankle, crumpled to the floor. He asked the defender if he had kicked him. When the answer was no, Kobe immediately suspected the worst—a ruptured Achilles tendon—and he was right. At first, he sat on the court trying to somehow press the tendon back into place with his hand. Remarkably, he refused help and shuffled off the court to the far bench for a timeout and then back to the free-throw line, where he swished two foul shots to tie the game, a simple but heroic action that still astounds athletes who've had this excruciatingly painful injury.

With Kobe unable to run, the Lakers intentionally fouled after the free throws to stop the action and he walked off the court under his own power. His mission was cut short, but accomplished. The Lakers won the game. He would play only six games the following season and would never play in the postseason again, but on the strength of his superhuman run, L.A. made the playoffs.

Some blamed the injury on the team for playing him beyond normal limits. Some blamed him for pushing himself too hard. Most people accepted that the whole situation was just Kobe being Kobe. "People can say he was stubborn, but his stubbornness for that many years has led him to greatness," teammate Darius Morris said. "It's kind of like the gift and curse of being Kobe Bryant."

CHOOSE TENACITY

Playing basketball, for Kobe, was do or die; it was all-out war. "I always aimed to kill the opposition," he wrote in his book, *Mamba Mentality*. When facing Philly in a championship series, he vowed not to defeat them, but to "cut their hearts out," a line that earned him boos in his hometown for the rest of his career. The toughness was no act. He knew how to push through pain. He won his last NBA championship with a painful, badly broken finger. He adjusted his shot and got on with winning.

When Kobe tore his right rotator cuff, he stayed in the game and started shooting left-handed, with this explanation: "God gave us two hands." When he needed surgery for that injury, he shocked observers by shooting jumpers just before the operation, saying "it doesn't really hurt that bad."

The filmmaker Gotham Chopra, who chronicled one of Kobe's last seasons in the documentary *Muse,* was shocked by his dedication and pace. Their first meeting was scheduled for August 23rd, Kobe's birthday. This initially surprised Chopra, who thought the star might take the day off to treat himself and enjoy his family. But in the months that followed, as he and his camera crew chased after Kobe and followed his exhausting schedule, Chopra learned how he liked to spend his time. It turns out, work itself was Kobe's treat. "He just has this relentlessness that is both exhilarating and exhausting at the same time," Chopra explained.

"YOU ALWAYS BET ON THE ONE THAT EATS, SLEEPS, AND BREATHES THE CRAFT."

"THE STRUGGLES TO GET THERE—THAT COMPLETES THE JOURNEY. IT'S THE UGLY MOMENTS THAT CREATE THE BEAUTY. THOSE ARE THE MOMENTS I TRULY APPRECIATE."

STAT ⚡ Combining regular season and playoffs, Kobe played more minutes of NBA basketball than any guard ever, logging more than 57,000 minutes in his 1,566 career games.

Kobe considered his unrelenting approach a simple choice that anyone could make:

"No matter what you do, if you want to be a basketball player, if you want to be a writer, if you want to be a TV host—or whatever it is that you want to do—it's making sure that you focus with laser-like precision on that goal."

He respected workhorses, not show horses: "If you're going to bet," he said, "you got to bet on the horse that you know is obsessive about what they do, day in and day out, and is going to be hell bent on trying to win a championship." Kobe knew that success wasn't beyond anyone's reach; that it simply required the kind of drive he was born with.

USE ALL THE TIME YOU HAVE

In his playing career, Kobe would usually wake early and go to bed late. In between, there would be multiple sessions to work on his skills and strength, plus countless hours studying his opponents and himself on video. This was all in addition to team practices and, of course, the games themselves—punishing battles against some of the world's toughest athletes. His teammate Pau Gasol recounted how the Lakers gathered for a team dinner at the end of the regular season one year. It was a chance for the squad to bond and relax before the high-pressure playoffs began. Late that night, as the other players left the dinner and went home, Kobe headed to the gym for his third workout of the day. He was in full competition mode, as usual. Of Kobe Bryant, Gasol said:

"In my entire career, I've never seen a player as dedicated to being the best. His determination is unparalleled. He unquestionably worked harder than anyone else I have ever played with. Kobe knew that to be the best, you need a different approach from everyone else."

Scores of teammates and competitors have similar recollections. His longtime coach, Phil Jackson, remembers regularly showing up at the Lakers facility on game or practice days at 8:30 a.m. for a staff meeting with his coaches. "More often than not," Jackson recalled, "by the time I pulled in, Kobe would already be parked in the car next to my designated spot, taking a nap." He had arrived before 6 a.m., completed his own personal workout, and was resting up for the Lakers' regular practice. "Kobe led by example for his teammates," Jackson said. "They couldn't keep up—but they were always challenged by the example he set."

O. J. Mayo was the top high school player in America and attending the Kobe Bryant Basketball Academy when he asked if he and his hero could work out together. Kobe agreed, and said he'd pick Mayo up at three. The next evening, Mayo asked Kobe why he never showed up. "Three in the morning," Kobe clarified. "Not three in the afternoon."

One coach, Eric Musselman, also remembers how Kobe liked to get an edge while his opponents were sleeping. He recalls leaving the Lakers practice facility near

"PRACTICE MAKES PERMANENT."

"GOD BLESSED ME WITH THE ABILITY TO DO THIS. I'M NOT GOING TO SHORTCHANGE THAT BLESSING."

midnight and finding Kobe in the parking lot; he had been waiting for the last person to leave. Once he confirmed with the coach that the gym was completely empty, Kobe slipped in. He wasn't showing off his dedication. In fact, he preferred to keep it quiet and to avoid distractions when he practiced. "He did not want anyone in that gym. He did not want anyone to see him going in," Musselman recalls. "It was just him and the security guard."

DO MORE

When he first joined the Lakers, before training camp even began,

Kobe's teammates noticed something remarkable about the teenager's energy level. In one day, he might practice against L.A. pros, then go to local Palisades High School to practice some more, and then test himself against college players at UCLA. "He was putting himself through three practices a day and practicing against every level of player," said teammate Cedric Ceballos. "A lot of guys thought no way he should be practicing that much, but he was 17." The Lakers were only beginning to witness Kobe's spectacular work ethic.

"MY ROUTINE WAS GRUELING. IT INVOLVED STRETCHING, LIFTING, TRAINING, HOOPING, RECOVERY, AND FILM STUDY."

It wasn't just youthful exuberance; for the next 20 years, Kobe kept it up. During the off-season, he followed what he called the "six-six-six program," working out for six hours a day, six days a week, over six months. The six hours were often broken up into two hours of running, two hours of weightlifting, and two hours of hoops. Typical sessions would begin at 5 a.m., 11 a.m., and 6 p.m., with 15-minute naps tucked into the day as needed. He particularly liked the 5 a.m. workouts, a habit he had picked up in high school. "By starting earlier, I set myself up for an extra workout each day," he noted. "Over the course of the summer, that's a lot of extra hours in the gym." By his calculations, he had found a way to squeeze more out of every 24 hours.

With his wiry frame, he had to work hard to be strong enough for the NBA. At 6-foot-6, he played at a lean 212 pounds, and it took consistent workouts to turn him into a fairly well-muscled pro. Former coach and NBA executive Stu Jackson said Kobe was the rare player who worked even harder on himself after making it big: "He committed himself to continually changing his body." His weight training program was old-school and remarkably intense, with a focus on basic lifting and muscle strengthening. A typical upper-body routine would include classics such as the bench press, lat pull-down, incline press, military press, bicep curls, and push-ups. "If something has worked for other greats before you, and if something is working for you," he reasoned, "why change it up and embrace some new fad?" He knew that if he trained hard using the basics, he could get his body where he wanted it to be.

PREPARE TO WIN

Late in any game's final minutes, when everyone else was diminished by exhaustion, Kobe felt confident that his training had prepared him. He loved hitting his signature clutch shots. When they went in, he'd be the hero. When they didn't, he was criticized for his hubris. But these bold and improbable shots were

"A BIG SHOT IS JUST ANOTHER SHOT. IF YOU MAKE A THOUSAND SHOTS A DAY, IT'S JUST ONE OF A THOUSAND. ONCE YOU'RE HITTING THAT MANY, WHAT'S ONE MORE?"

never as wild as they seemed. They were part of his pregame routine, rehearsed many hours before the game even began. "People don't realize," explained former Lakers assistant coach Brian Shaw, "he actually practiced those crazy shots." On game days, he typically would begin his pregame shooting routine four hours before tip-off, making 250 shots in 20 to 30 minutes. On nongame days, he liked to make 500 shots in about an hour. He believed in repetition.

For Kobe, practice was church, and he was a devout worshipper. He not only prepared for the big moments; he mastered the small ones. Alone in a gym, he would repeat moves endlessly. He'd work on his up-and-under step-through post-up move until it was as natural as a simple layup. His approach was to prepare as if his skills were lacking and then perform as if he were legendary. "He worked as if he wasn't very good," said NBA guard Spencer Dinwiddie. "But then he got on the court, he carried himself like, 'No, I'm the best and baddest person on the planet and can't nobody stop anything that I want to do.'"

While he knew how to get himself ready, it drove him crazy when others did not take their preparation as seriously. Even in high school practices, nothing was casual for him. During one seemingly insignificant three-on-three drill, a high school teammate named Rob Schwartz, who was a nonstarter on the team and almost a foot shorter than Kobe, missed a layup to cost their team a chance to win the drill. "Most kids go to the water fountain and move on," said his high school coach Gregg Downer. But Kobe chased down Schwartz in the hallway and scolded him for causing the defeat. Schwartz recalled the moment years later: "It was like, by losing that drill, I'd lost us the state championship."

JUMP AT A CHALLENGE

The Sixers regularly held practice at a nearby college campus, and even before he had started his senior year of high school, Kobe

"IF SOMEBODY'S NOT OBSESSED WITH WHAT THEY DO, WE DON'T SPEAK THE SAME LANGUAGE."

was invited to play against top college prospects that the team was considering for the draft. He had a useful habit of maximizing such opportunities. Knowing he was lucky to be inside the gym of an NBA practice, he hung around after his workouts were over. He was eager to take on challenges, even dunking on Sixers center Shawn Bradley, who at 7-foot-6, was a full foot taller than him. With his typical audacity, he challenged members of the Sixers to one-on-one games, including Jerry Stackhouse, a young star who had been the league's No. 3 overall pick a year earlier. These games mattered desperately to him, and

he went at it hard. Just as with his childhood H-O-R-S-E game against Brian Shaw, he insisted for the rest of his life that he never lost to Stackhouse. "Not once," he said, citing two coaches by name who could verify his account if Stackhouse "tries to lie."

Kobe never stopped competing and challenging others. He was constantly trying to persuade people to play against him. "We'd play games of one-on-one to a hundred," his high school teammate Schwartz said. "Sometimes he'd score 80 points before I got one basket. I think the best I ever did was to lose a hundred to 12."

"I'M NOT A PLAYER
THAT IS JUST GOING
TO COME AND GO.
I'M NOT A PLAYER
THAT IS GOING TO MAKE
AN ALL-STAR TEAM
ONE TIME, TWO TIMES.
I'M HERE TO BE AN
ALL-TIME GREAT."

As his high school career ended, Kobe took his ferocious attitude to a gym in Los Angeles to work out for Jerry West, who was not only a legendary former Laker but in the midst of becoming perhaps the greatest general manager in NBA history. West put him through a tough workout, asking him to play against a top defender, former Laker Michael Cooper. There was also a one-on-one matchup with a tough college star who had first-round NBA talent, Dontaé Jones. *Sports Illustrated* described the way Kobe handled this challenge: "A ball was tossed between them, and everyone stood back. Bryant devoured the moment smoothly, like a lion with excellent table manners." The performance was so dominating that West left the tryout early, telling a colleague with a quiet chuckle, "I've seen enough." Kobe's relentless approach had paid off. Weeks later, West engineered the draft-day trade for him, later saying he was the best prospect he had ever put through a workout.

LESSONS FROM A LEGEND

- WHEN YOU FIND SOMETHING THAT YOU'RE GOOD AT, GET EVEN BETTER.

- USE TIME LIKE A WEAPON. WORK LONGER THAN YOUR COMPETITORS.

- WHEN EVERYTHING'S ON THE LINE, GO HARDER.

- PREPARE AS IF YOU'RE ORDINARY. PERFORM AS IF YOU'RE LEGENDARY.

KEEP LEARNING

Kobe arrived in the NBA as a largely unknown quantity with a lot to learn. Other top draft picks become stars in college, having played on the national stage during the March Madness of the NCAA basketball tournament. He came from the small suburban gym at Lower Merion High School. For NBA fans, his potential was more rumor than fact. Most insiders who observed him during his first season agreed that this 18-year-old wasn't ready for the NBA.

At Lakers camp, players and coaches considered him talented, but very green, a ball hog who didn't understand the team concept. To make matters worse, his cocksure ways grated on almost everyone. When asked about his goals by a teammate, he blankly put out there:

"I want to be the best player in the league." Coming from a teenager in a locker room of veteran players, that level of arrogance did nothing to endear the rookie to his new team. He thought he was good enough to start, and told his coaches that he could outplay

PROM KING

In high school, Kobe gained some national notoriety for his basketball exploits, but he was more widely known for his prom date than his jump shot. He had met the pop singer and TV star Brandy at an award show and, with his usual confidence, brazenly asked her to his prom. She accepted, and they later attended his high school dance together, causing a stir when their white limo was greeted by reporters and shrieks from Brandy's excited young fans.

anybody in the NBA. The coaches assured him that he couldn't, but as they saw his frustration grow, they could tell that their message wasn't getting through. Their joke was that Kobe could speak multiple languages but couldn't hear in any of them.

The reviews from Lakers camp weren't stellar. His head coach, Del Harris, called Kobe a kid in a man's game, and said the teen would be better off on a team that wasn't trying to win a championship. His high school squad had revolved around him, but the NBA was different.

Meanwhile, other rookie guards were making a huge splash in the league. Allen Iverson scored 30 points in his debut game, and averaged 23.5 for the season. By comparison, Kobe didn't score at all in his first game, and played only six minutes. He averaged 7.6 points per game for the season. Iverson was an instant star; an exciting, authentic hip-hop hero for a new generation of NBA fans, while Kobe was less relatable. He was seen as a privileged and perhaps overrated player with an NBA dad and a distant, European background. Stung by the criticism, Kobe faced his first professional crisis. He was being overshadowed and outdone. His solution was to throw himself into learning everything he could about the NBA game and to set some long-term goals for his own improvement:

> **"MY FOCUS WAS JUST ALL ON IMPROVING AND GETTING BETTER. I NEVER REALLY CAME UP FOR AIR, BECAUSE I WAS JUST CONSTANTLY GOIN', GOIN', GOIN'."**

"You focus on one or two things throughout the summer. You master those things. Then the following summer, you focus on another one or two things. . . . Five years from now, you have a game that has no weaknesses in it."

The payoff did take time. It wasn't until his third year that Kobe's coaches believed he understood and embraced the concept of team basketball. After that season, Phil Jackson became the Lakers coach, and was instantly impressed by how much this young star had learned. The player and coach immediately started detailed discussions about Jackson's complex triangle offense. "He was already a student of the game and had studied various aspects of the offense," Jackson said. "Here he was, 20 years old, sounding like he'd been a pro for a decade."

ASK QUESTIONS
Kobe's personality was a unique mix of cocky and curious. While he saw

FIRST LESSON

Kobe's favorite children's book was *Curious George*. He identified with George's tireless quest to know more. Later, indulging his own curiosity helped him constantly improve.

himself as having almost limitless capabilities, he was always in search of an edge. So, he embarked on a lifelong quest to discover as much as he could. In search of even tiny details that could help him improve, Kobe would talk to anyone, whether it was an opponent, a teammate, a former player, or a coach. "I asked a ton of questions," he recalled. "I was genuinely thirsty to hear their answers and glean new info." He had discussions with old-time hoop stars such as Jerry West and Oscar Robertson, who gave him useful tips and helped him pick up good habits. Some of his contemporaries turned down his requests and didn't want to share secrets. That didn't deter Kobe. He would just move on to the next guy.

Michael Jordan was one of the players who wasn't thrilled to

share all of his secrets, but that didn't stop Kobe from pressing him for inside tips anyway. Once, when the clock had stopped for a foul shot, a young Kobe had the temerity to probe Jordan for advice midgame. He surprised the star athlete by asking about the release angle on his fadeaway jumper. Jordan, who was 15 years older, couldn't help but appreciate the audacity and specificity of the question. He answered the question and ultimately adopted Kobe as something of a protégé, sharing insight often throughout his career.

DO YOUR HOMEWORK

Kobe's interest in self-improvement started when he was a boy analyzing the styles of the NBA's biggest stars. Reviewing game tapes helped him become more familiar with the best elements of the greatest players.

"MY PHILOSOPHY
SEEMS LIKE A
PRETTY SIMPLE
ONE, BUT JUST
LIVE YOUR
LIFE TO GET
BETTER EVERY
SINGLE DAY."

"IT'S REALLY ABOUT WANTING TO LEARN, AND FEELING LIKE YOUR CUP IS ALWAYS EMPTY, BECAUSE THERE'S ALWAYS MORE THAT YOU CAN FILL IT WITH."

Some of his favorites: "Magic Johnson's backdoor moves. Hakeem [Olajuwon]'s post up. Michael Jordan's quickness."

Once in the league, his obsession with video study continued. At first, he simply watched the games as they were. As his expertise grew, he began to see the action as it should have unfolded, imagining the alternatives and countermoves that would have led to better results. At halftime, he would watch clips of the game's first two quarters. On off days, he might spend up to five hours analyzing the details of a single game, or combing over tapes of old-school legends like Pete Maravich. He didn't just watch other superstars play. He made it his job to study them. He liked to say that some players enjoy looking at a watch. Others, like him, need to know how the watch works.

NOTICE EVERYTHING

Kobe became obsessed with the angles of basketball, and how even a slight change of location on the court altered a player's line of attack. He watched players' shoulders, feet, and head positioning, and the subtle ways that some could balance their weight without signaling their intentions. Unlike many young players, he also focused on defense. As soon as he joined the Lakers, he asked for video footage of the guards he would be facing to help him prepare. He also sought out Gary Payton, Scottie Pippen, Eddie Jones, and other great defenders for advice. Through the years, he kept at it. When prepping to go against an opponent, he would sometimes watch that team's five previous games, rewinding, pausing, and rewinding again until their movements and tendencies were imprinted on his brain.

The education paid off—he became one of the best defensive players in the league. Coaches noted that he often understood an opposing team's offense as well or better than the team itself. He would talk at length and in detail about how to defend rival players, and that included Allen Iverson. When the two stars met in the NBA finals in their fifth season, it was clear that Kobe had surpassed his rival's place in the league. He convincingly won his second championship, putting him on top of the basketball world.

WORK WELL WITH OTHERS

Of course, he didn't reach such heights on his own. For the first eight years of his career, he was famously paired with one of the best big men in NBA history. At 7-foot-1 and 325 pounds, Shaquille O'Neal was larger than life, with a loose approach, a magnetic personality and a fearsome reputation. The relationship between the two men was arguably the most analyzed and mercurial player partnership in American sports history. When it worked well, it was sublime,

STAT ⚡ **Known for his offense, Kobe learned to be a great defender and was named to the NBA all-defensive first team nine times.**

"IT NEVER BOTHERED
ME WHEN PEOPLE
WOULD SAY, 'YOU ONLY
WIN CHAMPIONSHIPS
BECAUSE YOU'RE
PLAYING WITH SHAQ.'
IT BOTHERED ME
WHEN *HE* SAID IT."

producing a substantial highlight reel of championships and thrilling dominance. They were true opposites. While Kobe was a loner who shunned the Hollywood spotlight, Shaq was drawn to it. Kobe made it known that he appreciated O'Neal taking center stage: "It's actually perfect." he said. "I can learn every facet of the game without everyone analyzing every move I make."

Their different personalities, however, didn't always mesh. The two egos and work styles clashed, leading Kobe to face one of the biggest challenges and learning opportunities of his career. His frustration would sometimes descend into childish name-calling: Kobe publicly chided Shaq for being out of shape, for sitting out with minor injuries, and for caring more about money than winning. Shaq was annoyed by his hard-driving teammate. Many thought he was also jealous of Kobe's immense popularity with Laker fans. At its worst, it turned physical: Shaq once slapped Kobe in the face during a particularly contentious practice when Kobe was 20. At another infamous scrimmage, the two athletes squared off and fought. O'Neal threw a hard punch that partially landed before the two were pulled apart.

By the time Kobe reached his fifth year in the league, he had become one of the league's best players and craved a bigger role. The Lakers were already world champions, but he wasn't satisfied. He wanted to supplant Shaq as the team leader, and old resentments and frustrations deepened the rift between the two players. That season, Jackson asked Kobe to run

---

STAT ⚡ **Kobe's NBA debut in 1996 was historic: At 18 years and 72 days old, he was—at the time—the youngest player to make an NBA game appearance.**

---

the offense through Shaq, except for late in the game when O'Neal's poor foul-shooting could prove risky. In the coach's plan, those final minutes would be Kobe's main opportunity to take over. The young buck wasn't buying. "Turn my game down? I need to turn it up," he said at the time. "I've improved. How are you going to bottle me up? I'd be better off playing someplace else." Sharing the spotlight was not working for him.

Leaving for another team wasn't a new consideration. Despite going 67-15 in 1999–2000 and winning three NBA titles in their tenure together, both players regularly requested trades. "If leaving the Lakers at the end of the season is what I decide, a major reason will be Shaq's childlike selfishness and jealousy," Kobe said in 2003. But in the end, the Lakers made their choice: The following summer, Shaq's trade request was finally granted, breaking up the duo.

The difficulties with O'Neal may have challenged Kobe, but they also chastened him and taught him lessons that shaped the final decade of his career. For one, he ultimately came to realize that when you're surrounded by talent, different approaches are to be expected and accepted:

> *"Sports are such a great teacher. I think of everything they've taught me: camaraderie, humility, how to resolve differences. Playing with Shaq made me understand that you're never going to change a person. You have to be open-minded and not be rigid. If you're rigid, that's weakness."*

"THE IMPORTANT THING IS YOU CONTINUE TO GROW."

After Shaq left, Kobe got his wish to become the Lakers' team leader, a status he held for the rest of his career. That first summer, he prepared by adding 15 pounds of muscle, knowing that he would be handling a heavier workload. He remained hypercompetitive, but coaches and players noticed some subtle shifts. While he bristled at being coached early in his career, he ultimately came to show respect and appreciation for Jackson, whose understated, consistent techniques complemented his own methodical approach.

BE REAL

Out from Shaq's shadow, Kobe was more mature and more attuned to his teammates' needs. It started with self-reflection. He knew that other players were intimidated by his reputation and found his demanding personality difficult to work with. Early in his career, he had hidden any self-doubt under a veneer of invincibility, but now he saw how that cockiness had made it harder to connect with teammates. It didn't come naturally to him, but

for the good of the team, he began opening up and sharing stories of his own struggles and doubts.

Shaq and Kobe eventually reconciled, and Kobe regretted how hardheaded he had been. "When you get older," he said, "you have more perspective, and you're like, 'Holy [expletive]. I was an idiot when I was a kid.'" But remnants of the rivalry never left him. Ever the scorekeeper, he was proud that he continued elevating his game and won two championships after their breakup, while Shaq only won one. O'Neal retired after 19 seasons. Kobe played 20. As he got older, he liked outlasting his contemporaries. "I take a lot of pride at being able to do what I do at this level for so many years," he admitted.

FIGURE IT OUT

As Kobe changed and improved throughout his basketball years, one particular ability aided him greatly: He was an amazingly quick study. Thirteen years into his career, he flew to Texas to spend a day at the ranch of the great retired

"I STARTED TO UNDERSTAND THAT MY TEAMMATES VIEWED ME LIKE SOME DAMN MACHINE."

Hall of Fame center, Hakeem Olajuwon, to work on perfecting his footwork and post up moves. Over many years, Olajuwon taught lots of players, most of them centers, but he called Kobe the best student he ever had. Olajuwon would teach a move and watch in amazement as Kobe executed it perfectly. Teammates also marveled that he could try a complicated new move in practice, stay late to get his footwork right, then spring it publicly—and successfully—in an NBA game the next night. "I've never seen somebody who can see a move that another guy does and learn it as quickly as he can," Robert Horry said.

His penchant for learning wasn't limited to the court. When he got married, Kobe, who already spoke English and Italian, taught himself Spanish to communicate better with his Mexican American mother-in-law. Later, in his mid-30s during a rough patch in his marriage, he decided he wanted to play Beethoven's "Moonlight Sonata" on the piano as a grand, romantic gesture to surprise his wife. He chose that song because, as he explained, "There's so much beauty and agony [in it]." His only problem was this: He had no idea how to play the piaNo. He thought taking lessons would be too easy, too ordinary, and would somehow cheapen the gift. Instead, he taught himself by ear, working countless hours at a keyboard with the song playing on a loop in his headphones. According to Kobe, "If you just sit down and say, 'I'm going to learn this thing until I do,' there's not really much out there that you can't figure out eventually." And he did.

CULTIVATE MENTORS

Whether it was basketball or the world of multimedia storytelling, Kobe gained mastery by asking questions of anyone who would take his call. And when they didn't take his call, he'd call back, sometimes daily. He hounded J.K. Rowling until she agreed to get together with him and discuss story construction. He talked to actors about how they made characters come to life. He quizzed producers about how to lead a creative effort. He called Steven Spielberg. He went to lunch with John Williams, the famed film-score composer, and asked how he built crescendos into his pieces. He asked Oprah Winfrey how she built a studio. And when he wanted to understand how to create a fantasy universe, he tracked down George R.R. Martin, who wrote the novels that became *Game of Thrones*.

Kobe could work on his own when he needed to, but he believed that to excel in any field it was critical to find successful mentors and learn from their advice and example. "There's always a common thread," he said, referring to those who

"I HAD TO EXPLAIN THAT I HAD THE SAME FEARS, FLAWS, VULNERABILITIES, SO THEY COULD RELATE TO ME."

made their mark. "There's always a common denominator between what has made people great, and what has separated good from great." Probing successful people for tidbits of wisdom could help him develop similar habits and approaches and enable him to make the leap to greatness.

His first mentor was his dad, Joe. Growing up, Kobe idolized him, learning invaluable fundamentals and toughness from him. Their one-on-one games were the stuff of family lore, with the son battling hard and the father coming back harder—in some cases ripping open his son's lip with a thrown elbow. Kobe finally won a game against his dad for the first time when he was 16, only a year before being drafted by the Lakers.

LEARN FROM THE BEST

Just a couple of years later, Kobe was a young pro in Los Angeles when he began learning from a very different kind of mentor. It started with a phone call in the summer after his first season. He was lifting weights at the Gold's Gym in Venice, California, when his cell phone rang. It was Michael Jackson. The music legend was calling out of the blue. He had read about the Laker's work ethic and ambition, and wanted to tell him he was on the right course. He said he saw greatness in him. "Keep doing what you're doing," Jackson encouraged him. "Don't come back to the pack and be normal for the sake of blending in with others. Don't dumb it down."

And so began one of Kobe's most surprising and important relationships. "Michael Jackson was probably the biggest mentor I ever had. That phone call in Gold's Gym," said Kobe, "literally changed my life." In subsequent conversations and visits, Jackson shared the process and details for how he made his music. He told Kobe that his curiosity would be his greatest gift, and that he should use it to expand his vision of what's possible. He advised him to learn from the greats, and find out what worked for them and what didn't. Jackson said he recognized Kobe's "insatiable thirst for excellence," and assured him that while his approach would bring critics, he should never let that derail him. He also shared books with Kobe, including Napoleon Hill's *Success Through a Positive Mental Attitude*.

In Michael Jackson, Kobe saw a loner like himself who was able to use his obsessive drive to reach the highest levels of his profession, his way. Jackson told him how he had ached to create the best-selling album ever. At the time, the *Saturday Night Fever* soundtrack was the all-time No. 1 seller, so Jackson listened to it, over and over—10 times a day for two years, trying to discern its magic. A few years later, he released *Thriller*, which sold 60 million copies and became the greatest selling album in history. For Kobe, this was a revelation. "I [expletive] love that story," he would often say about about how obsessiveness turned Jackson into the King of Pop. In fact, that story became a map for the tunnel-vision path that he would follow for the rest of his life: "It was all the validation that I needed—to know that I had to focus on my craft and never waver."

LESSONS FROM A LEGEND

- DO YOUR HOMEWORK. STUDY HARD.
- MAKE CONSTANT IMPROVEMENT THE GOAL.
- TURN TOUGH SITUATIONS INTO LEARNING OPPORTUNITIES.
- REACH OUT FOR ADVICE FROM SUCCESSFUL PEOPLE.

TRAIN YOUR MIND

By the NBA's unparalleled athletic standards, Kobe Bryant's body was nothing special. He was fast but not blazing. His 40-inch vertical leap was ordinary, not mind-blowing. His hands were large, not massive. But his mind was elite. His teammates, coaches, and other close observers saw his mental edge as his superpower. He was extremely smart, but he had something else beyond intelligence—a level of mental fortitude rarely seen. It was a formidable force that fueled his rise and helped make him an all-time great.

When he retired, basketball fans and players recalled the championships and the dramatic flair and artistry of Kobe's game. But more than anything, they remembered the mental rigor. His fierce confidence and incredible discipline on the court. His ability to live in the moment and make it his. His unflappable focus on process and results. His deftness at analyzing problems and figuring out solutions. This is what other coaches feared most when playing the Lakers. "It's what set him apart," said Gregg Popovich, coach

"NO MATTER WHAT, I UNDERSTOOD THAT I COULD LOSE MYSELF IN THE GAME."

of the San Antonio Spurs. "He seems to understand what the game demands, and there are very, very few people in the league who can do that, and he does it better than anyone."

Among his mental powers was his ability to find focus amid the chaos. Whether the Lakers were competing for a championship or struggling, his mindset didn't waver:

> *"I had to figure out how to steel my mind and keep calm and centered. That's not to say my emotions didn't spike or drop here or there, but I was aware enough to recalibrate and bring them back level before things spiraled. I could do that in a way others couldn't, and that was really key for me."*

GET IN THE ZONE

Hours before a game would begin, long before the crowd arrived, Kobe could be found by himself, in the quiet, empty arena, shooting. Alone on the hardwood, it all felt perfect: "It's just me and the basket, the court, and my imagination, dreams. It gives me a sense of nirvana." For Kobe, the loner, preparing in solitude kept his mind clear, and ready for the game to come:

> *"When I jogged out of the tunnel and the fans were screaming and it's loud, the noise didn't impact me. Mentally, I was able to remember the stillness of the earlier moment and carry that with me."*

As the game drew closer, like most players, he listened to music on his headphones in the training room. His first step was to gauge himself and match his playlist to his needs. When he wanted to get fired up, he played hard-edge hip-hop. His favorite album was Jay-Z's *Reasonable Doubt*, but he also loved *Life After Death* by Biggie Smalls. Other times he turned to rock bands such as the Red Hot Chili Peppers and Nirvana. If he felt like he was too keyed up, he would soothe himself with familiar songs from his high school game bus, or ones that reminded him of his childhood in Italy. He said it transported his mind back to those simpler times. "It's not just listening to music to listen to music," he explained, "but whatever music's going to put me in the right emotional setting that I feel is important to that game." When the moment called for silence, he just wore the headphones for solitude and let the quiet move him.

His music choices could be unique. For example, he'd sometimes prepare by listening to the ominous, thumping theme from the horror movie *Halloween*. In a sense, the music let him put on the mask of the film's murderous villain, Michael Myers. "It's just stone-cold killer," Kobe explained. "And I would listen to that song over and over. That's when you know you better run. It's going to be a tough night."

Right before tip-off, when the national anthem would play, Kobe would slip into an extraordinary meditative zone in his mind—a combination of concentration, peace, and hyperawareness. He would survey the baskets in front of him and behind him, and the teammates around him. He'd sense the vibe of the arena and try to be carried on the wavelength of that moment. "I'm trying to feel the energy of the environment and allow it to move through me," Kobe explained. "That then propels me and fuels me to have a great performance."

CHOOSE CONFIDENCE OVER FEAR

As he prepared his mind, he thought a lot about how to conquer doubts and worry. To Kobe, trying to be fearless was foolish. Fear was real. The goal was to overcome it. He remembered as a kid having to conquer his fear during karate lessons. He'd be matched against bigger, stronger, more experienced competition. He discovered that, even when he lost, the reality wasn't as bad as he had dreaded. The lesson stuck with him: Don't let your own mind be the enemy. Don't psyche yourself out before the battle even begins. "You're always dealing with fear," Kobe explained, "or with something in your imagination. Something that you think can happen. But you just say, 'I don't know if I can do that. But I'll give it a try.'" Confidence for Kobe was a choice he had to make again and again.

Over the course of a grueling NBA career, it wasn't always easy to believe in himself. "I have insecurity. I have fear of failure," he admitted at age 35 even after winning five championships. But Kobe knew that when you controlled your fear, good things would follow.

DISPLAY STRENGTH

The self-assuredness Kobe projected was one of his most distinctive characteristics. In his first all-star game, when Kobe was 19, Karl Malone tried to set a screen for him, but he directed Malone out of the way so that he could try to score on Jordan one-on-one. Malone,

"WE ALL HAVE SELF-DOUBT. YOU DON'T DENY IT, BUT YOU ALSO DON'T CAPITULATE TO IT. YOU EMBRACE IT. YOU RISE ABOVE IT."

"IF YOU DON'T BELIEVE IN YOURSELF, NO ONE WILL DO IT FOR YOU."

one of the most accomplished and physically imposing players in league history, couldn't believe the young player's audacity, complaining later that if he's going to get waved around the court by a teenager, he'd rather not even play. Other all-stars were also shocked at Kobe's gall. His reputation for cockiness sprung from such moments, but he didn't mind—he liked that his rivals saw him as fearless.

In the first half of his career, he was considered obstinate and hard to handle. In 2005, after years of butting heads with Kobe, Phil Jackson called him uncoachable. Much later, Kobe looked back on his youthful attitude. "Most successful people are a little arrogant. I was very stubborn," he admitted, comparing himself to a

wild horse that needed taming. Still, he recognized that his raw fury was part of what made him special. As his career advanced, he found ways to get along better with others, but he always retained the swagger that made him Kobe.

FIND WHAT MOTIVATES YOU

Kobe believed the competitor with the mental advantage generally wins and would use whatever tricks he could find to give himself that edge. In 2008, the rival Celtics beat the Lakers for the NBA title, embarrassing them by 39 points in the final game. He walked off the court feeling dejected. The fans in Boston were delirious with celebration and the Journey song, "Don't Stop Believin'" blared. Instead of wishing this difficult moment away,

Kobe kept it with him and used it as a source of motivation. For the next two years, that song was a mainstay on his pregame playlist. He listened to it every day to relive the pain and humiliation of the defeat. Powered by the memory, he led the Lakers to titles in each of those two seasons, including a revenge championship against Boston in 2010.

KEEP YOUR COOL

One of Kobe's most enduring mental tricks was his ability to simplify a pressure-filled situation. When fear of failure crept in, his old gym at Lower Merion would go through his mind and he would pretend that he was still in high school, just trying to get his team to the state championship. "It's just playing with insanely more talented players and competition," he said of the difference between an NBA game and a high school game. "Everything else is the same."

In the deciding seventh game against the Celtics in those 2010 finals, he shot poorly as the Lakers fell behind by 13 points and seemed headed to what would have been the most painful loss of his career. In many ways, this was the biggest game he ever played. It was the only time he ever participated in a winner-take-all contest for an NBA championship. It was also against the Lakers' most hated foe, and with no Shaq to lean on, his individual legacy was on the line. But throughout his career, especially in the biggest moments, he had the ability to quiet his mind and surgically attack his opponent's weakness. Now, even as the game started to fall apart, he stayed calm, scoring 10 points in the fourth quarter to lead the comeback and win the title.

Like many great athletes, he could drum up motivation from almost anything, and use it effectively.

The day that LeBron James surpassed him to become the youngest player to reach 5,000 career points, the 21-year-old James punctuated the accomplishment with a 51-point game. The young phenom was the talk of the league. Kobe heard the chatter. The next night, he dropped 81.

Kobe got more all-star votes than any other player four times, and his jersey was among the best-selling for most of his career. But because of his killer instinct and repeated successes, he also was simultaneously one of the league's most hated players. Away from home, he liked to use the crowd's hostility as fuel to help him get the mental edge he craved. "It felt good going on the road," he said during one tough series in front of 36,000 loud, booing fans in San Antonio. "Going in there and taking care of business. That felt good."

Even in his hometown, he had to face some haters. A year after the Lakers beat the Sixers in the finals, the all-star game was played in Philadelphia. He expected a warm reception, but the crowd was still bitter about his take-no-prisoners comments during the finals, and loudly booed him every time he touched the ball. He later admitted that it was hurtful, but he didn't dwell on it. He said he had long ago realized that not everybody is going to be a fan. Rather than worry about it, he used it to drive him. He said opposing fans didn't bother booing bad players. It was a sign of respect, and the jeers only made him stronger. He put it all in the memory bank to be withdrawn when needed.

GET AMPED UP

On January 22, 2006, Kobe went up against the Toronto Raptors in what would be his most famous game. He kept his mental discipline as he made a remarkable 28 out of 46 shots and 18 of 20 from the free-throw line on his way to scoring 81 points, the second-highest total in NBA history (after Wilt Chamberlain's mind-blowing 100-point game in 1962.) He was always looking for reasons to get amped for a game, and that day was no different. It was the first NBA game his grandmother had ever seen in person. His wife and daughter would be there with her. It was also the birthday of his late grandfather, the man who had sent him NBA tapes when he was a kid living in Italy. This provided more grist for the mill churning in his mind. Rather than letting it all distract him, it inspired him.

LET IT FLOW

The 81 points were no fluke. He had been building toward this kind of monumental performance. A couple of weeks earlier, he scored 40 in the second half against the Clippers. The previous month, in just the first three quarters against Dallas, he personally outscored the entire Mavericks team 62 to 61 before sitting out the fourth quarter in a rout. But something else happened that month, too. Playing the woeful Raptors in Toronto, he scored a grand total of 11 points. Now, as the Lakers prepared to host that same weak Toronto team on January 22, he was thinking about redeeming himself. He was thinking about LeBron's 51 points the previous day. And about his lost grandfather, and his grandmother and family in the stands.

Then the game began. At first, his knees were tight and he played gingerly until, suddenly, shots began to fall. Something special was about to happen:

"I started getting in a rhythm, and the knees started loosening up, and then I just got on a roll. I didn't really pay attention to anything that was said. I was just in my own head and in my own zone. I wasn't high-fiving anybody. I wasn't talking to anybody. I wasn't worried about what was to come. I wasn't worried about what just happened. I was just here. I just felt like I was in a different dimension. Nothing else mattered."

FOCUS ON THE JOB

The Kobe mindset was a businesslike, no-nonsense attitude. Even his trash talking was strategic and economical. When interviewed, he might boast about destroying opponents, but once the game

"THESE YOUNG GUYS ARE PLAYING CHECKERS. I'M OUT THERE PLAYING CHESS."

began, he would settle into a clear-minded, competitive headspace and save his piercing words for the right moment. During the 2010 playoff run, he made an epic 3-pointer to end the hopes of the Phoenix Suns in the Western Conference finals, with defender Grant Hill closely guarding. As the ball went through the hoop, Kobe stepped backward over the sideline toward the Phoenix bench, and the Suns coach Alvin Gentry said, "Good defense, Grant." Kobe patted Gentry lightly on his rear end and responded, "Not good enough." If a young player got the best of him for a stretch, he would offer congratulations while there was still a quarter left to play. "You had a great game, young fella." The

message was unmistakable—play time was over. Kobe would then do his best to dominate the kid for the rest of the game.

Among the qualities that lead to success, none meant more to Kobe than mental toughness. A major part of it was never showing vulnerability to his rivals, no matter who they were. Early in his career, he noticed that some players were clearly in awe of Jordan, even when competing against him. They called him "Black Jesus" and gushed about his amazing performances. Kobe saw it as weakness and aggressively rejected that kind of hero worship. He respected, studied, and talked to Jordan to learn from him, but he

"WE DON'T GET TOO HIGH,
WE DON'T GET TOO LOW.
WE JUST COME IN, CUT YOUR
HEARTS OUT, AND GO HOME."

deferred to no one. On the court, he was interested in winning, not watching others win. Later in his career, once his own legend was secure, he noticed that some younger players looked at him with the same reverence once reserved for Jordan. And he still didn't like it. "It's no fun playing against players like that." He wanted the challenge of defeating a confident opponent.

NEVER FLINCH

During one all-star game, Kobe's friend Dwyane Wade inadvertently broke his nose. After the game, he made sure to greet Wade before he got treatment for the injury. He wouldn't let Wade see him wearing a bandage. If this reaction sounds old-school, it was (and so was Kobe). Back in high school, he had broken his nose in practice days before the state championship semifinal game. He was fitted with a mask, but he ripped it off in front of his team right before the game started and threw it against a wall, yelling "I'm not wearing this thing. Let's go to war!" He scored 39 points in a victory, and three days later, overcame an aggressive double-team designed to stop him, as Lower Merion won the state championship.

Backing down wasn't a Kobe characteristic. In a widely replayed moment in 2010, he was playing defense as Matt Barnes prepared to inbound the ball. Barnes faked as if he were going to drill the ball hard into Kobe's face from just inches away, a move expected to cause a reflexive recoil from the defender. Kobe didn't move. Even his stoic facial expression remained unchanged. In that moment, he once again demonstrated an immutable fact to the rest of the NBA: Kobe Bryant doesn't flinch.

USE YOUR BRAIN

He wasn't afraid to fight. He was once suspended for elbowing an opponent in the face not long after having done the same to another. But a substantial part of Kobe's edge was more cerebral than confrontational. In high school, he scored 1080 on his SAT exam, good enough for acceptance at most colleges in that era. He reveled in mental challenges and was incredibly analytical. One of his trainers, who also worked with Jordan, said the difference was that Michael just wanted to know which exercises to do. Kobe wanted to know why.

In fact, when Kobe discussed his professional approach, he often used the metaphor of a puzzle. To him, a job was fun if you were constantly trying to solve it, like a riddle. That's how he deciphered the great players he faced: "My goal was to figure you out. And to do that, to figure those puzzles out, I was willing to do way more than anyone else." Later, when he launched his studio, his approach to problem-solving was strikingly familiar. He would excitedly talk about finding the emotional truth of a character or story, and working with it until all the pieces would click into place.

STAY IN THE MOMENT

With so much of Kobe's game taking place in his head, there was always something a bit metaphysical, even spiritual about his methods. This might explain why, when Jackson, the contemplative Lakers coach

known as the "Zen Master," taught the Lakers to meditate, Kobe took to it so easily. He'd close his eyes, focus intensely on his own deep breaths, and let thoughts float by without engaging with them. Before long, he was meditating 10 to 15 minutes most mornings, and did so for the rest of his life.

On the court, he created a type of game-time trance that served him well. He had admired the composed demeanor of Jackson's Bulls teams, and now he knew their secret. The Lakers adopted the same mindset to establish a cocoon of concentration:

"We were never rattled, ever, because we were always in the moment....Always looking at the reality of the situation, and not letting our emotions cloud our execution. And that comes from being in that meditative state."

Like anyone who meditates, some mornings he found his mind drifting, almost always to basketball. But at some point, he began realizing that his mid-meditation daydreams were no longer about hoops. To a man obsessed with monitoring and improving himself, this was a major signal. His beat-up body might still be willing, but his mind was moving on. Not long after, as he was preparing for his 20th season, he announced his retirement. Following Phil Jackson's advice, he approached the year with the goal of savoring the little moments and appreciating each feeling as it came.

When the day finally arrived for his last professional game, emotions pinballed through his system. The next morning, there would be no more practice and the lifelong Catholic would head to his church to give thanks for his remarkable career. But first, there was a game to play. That night, it didn't take long for him to find the sweet, familiar ease that he had always known on the court. "The game started and I was acutely focused," said Kobe. "I was in the moment, and any small thoughts of it being the final game disappeared." For one last time, he got happily snared in the give-and-take action, in what he called the "game of chess" that he had been playing on an NBA court for so long. When it ended, he emerged from the reverie and returned to civilization with his 60 points and one last victory.

LESSONS FROM A LEGEND

- ⊕ USE WHATEVER YOU CAN TO GET AMPED AND MOTIVATED.
- ⊕ DON'T LET FEAR RUIN YOUR HARD WORK.
- ⊕ CREATE A SERENE MENTAL SPACE THAT ALLOWS YOU TO SUCCEED.

BE YOU

CHAPTER 6

In a world where most people row in the same direction, Kobe liked going his own way. He didn't mind being unique. In fact, he preferred it. He thought too many people settled for being like everyone else. To him, conformity was a danger, not a goal. If that made him weird, he was OK with it. You had a chance to write your own story in life, so why would you make it drab or common?

Of course, Kobe's story was anything but boring. Part of the secret was that he had faith in himself, and never worried much about what anyone else thought. Naysayers only motivated him. It didn't matter whether they called him a villain or a hero, he didn't care. They could mock him for making goofy kid shows with animal puppets—that didn't change his vision. They could laugh at the unusual stylings of his first signature shoes (astronaut shoes, some said). He would laugh, too. He'd throw on those kicks and laugh all the way to the NBA championship.

"YOU'VE GOT TO ASK YOURSELF WHAT'S TRULY GOING TO GET YOU UP IN THE MORNING AND WHAT'S GOING TO KEEP YOU UP AT NIGHT. WHEN YOU FIND WHAT THAT ANSWER IS, YOU STAY TRUE TO THAT."

He liked blockbuster movies and Broadway musicals. He appreciated poets like Walt Whitman. "I am large, I contain multitudes," Whitman wrote, and somehow that's a perfect description of Kobe. He did contain multitudes. He loved books, opera, theater, animation, amusement parks, and hip-hop. Contradictions didn't trouble him. He was a one-of-a-kind mix of ambitious and grounded, brash and serious, single-minded and endlessly curious. He was a guy who embraced change but stayed with the same team for 20 years. People around the globe recognized his face, but even his teammates didn't know him well. On the court, he was filled with bravado. Off it, he preferred slipping into the background.

Those who knew him best noticed something rare in Kobe. Despite all his various sides, he had an exceptional steadiness, as if his internal compass was set and couldn't be reoriented. He knew where he wanted to go and had a good idea of how to get there. He never chased other people's expectations or goals. He understood himself and made his life his own.

This was no small thing. When people would ask him for advice in striving to reach their goals, he underscored the importance of self-knowledge. Understanding your body and mind. Being honest with yourself about what you want. Identifying and improving weaknesses. He believed these were the cornerstones that formed a strong foundation for any smart athlete—or any successful person— including him. "I know who I am," he often said. It sounded so simple, yet he considered this fact crucial and indispensable.

TRUST YOURSELF

As the top high school player in the country, Kobe drew intense defensive attention in every game. But he welcomed it, and didn't allow it to derail him. He would let the game come to him, feeling the rhythm of the action as it developed. And then, when it mattered most, he would take over, releasing a torrent of long jumpers and spinning drives to win. During his time on the Lakers, these well-executed explosions became his signature. He specialized in stepping up, with no apologies. "We have to know our strengths and weaknesses," he explained. He was clutch, and he knew it.

His teammates mostly understood his need to be the late-game hero. Rick Fox said they learned to just get out the way and let it happen. At times, there was grumbling that maybe he wasn't sharing the ball enough and was trying to do too much. After all, statistically, he wasn't a great 3-point shooter. His career percentage was just under 33 percent, below mediocre in a league where the average hovers near 36 percent and the best long-range marksmen shoot in the 40s. Even in the playoffs, Kobe took nearly 900 3-pointers and made fewer than 300. But with a game on the line, he wasn't worried about numbers. He said he'd been hearing the same thing since he was 8 years old—that he shoots too much. He liked to respond to this critique by pointing out that "some people thought Mozart had too many notes in his compositions." As Kobe told it, young Mozart didn't care

if critics thought it was too many notes or too few. The composer said he used as many as necessary. Kobe said that answer worked for him, too.

Of course, comparing himself to a genius only underscored the sense that Kobe's ego was permanently inflamed, but that accusation never bothered him either. As a boy in Italy, he would talk about his NBA future, not as a dream but as a matter of fact. When other kids laughed, he would sign his name on

"I NEVER FELT OUTSIDE PRESSURE. THE EXPECTATIONS I PLACED ON MYSELF WERE HIGHER THAN WHAT ANYONE EXPECTED FROM ME."

a piece of paper and hand it to one of the kids. "You might want to hold onto this," he'd say.

At 17, he heard NBA executives telling him it was a terrible idea to leap directly from high school to the NBA. "I think it's a total mistake," said the Celtics' director of basketball development, Jon Jennings. Yes, 6-foot-11 Kevin Garnett had done it the previous year, but, Jennings said, "Kobe is no Kevin Garnett." Others agreed. The kid out of Lower Merion heard all of these negative voices, but in the end, he listened to his own. And later, when he needed motivation to beat Boston or Garnett, thinking back to his old skeptics provided more tinder for the fire.

CONQUER INHIBITIONS

Kobe lived life on his own wavelength. He was almost completely unflappable. It was hard to embarrass him, mostly because he had supreme confidence and was never overly concerned about other people's opinions. As an 18-year-old rookie, when he won the slam-dunk competition at the NBA all-star weekend in Cleveland, the skinny teenager showed off his modest muscles for the crowd. "I know I don't have much," he said that night, "but I decided to flex what I have." That same boldness drove him to relentlessly ask other players for advice, even when it might be awkward to do so. He explained his thinking this way: "I'd rather risk embarrassment now than be embarrassed later, when I've won zero titles." He figured the worst they could do was tell him was No. And at best, he could learn something that would help him improve.

Even the critics couldn't make him second-guess himself. When they complained that he didn't pass enough, Kobe explained that he considered a shot "an intentional pass to oneself." By that logic, each made shot was, according to Kobe, an assist. It was a unique way to see the game of basketball, but nobody ever accused Kobe of being ordinary.

While there was no doubt that Kobe took his work seriously,

he didn't always take himself so seriously, especially in the big moments. This is when we got a glimpse of Kobe without his game face. When the buzzer sounded and it was official that he won his first NBA championship, he wasn't striking a cool pose for the cameras. Instead, free of any inhibitions, he joyously and famously leapt into Shaq's embrace, wrapping his arms and legs around the big center like a kid jumping up on his daddy. Victory often had this kind of effect on him. Roughly 20 years later, when his favorite NFL team, the Philadelphia Eagles, won the Super Bowl, his wife, Vanessa, captured his giddy, screaming, jumping, dancing, prancing reaction (complete with their baby tucked under his arm) in a home video that instantly went viral.

Being himself meant trying things that other players wouldn't. He didn't worry about embarrassing himself when he took up tap dancing. His goal was to find something to help with repeated ankle sprains, one of which caused him to miss a critical game in the 2000 finals. He was rolling his ankles so often that he'd try anything to fix the problem. That summer, he started tap dancing to strengthen his joints. When people heard, they giggled at the thought of the 6-foot-6 basketball star in tap shoes. It felt more like an activity for

"IF YOU'RE AFRAID TO FAIL, THEN YOU'RE PROBABLY GOING TO FAIL."

LIVING BY HIS OWN RULES

Kobe's lifestyle was unusual for a famous athlete. Unlike most young millionaire superstars in the city, he lived with his parents until he got married. Teammates said they never saw him at popular clubs where almost all the athletes hung out. In fact, most said they never saw him anywhere except the gym.

a school kid than a premier athlete. He didn't care. Even though he later admitted to being a terrible tap dancer, it helped his body; his ankles got stronger and he never missed another finals game.

INDULGE YOUR INTERESTS

When your first name comes from the Kobe Japanese Steak House and Sushi Bar in King of Prussia, Pennsylvania (and your middle name is Bean after your dad's hoop alias, "Jellybean"), it's unlikely you'll turn out to be an average guy. And Kobe never was.

Like his teammates, he loved to read *Slam* magazine and *Sports Illustrated*, but unlike them, he also studied a wide variety of thinkers and blended them into a unique

personal perspective. As hard as it was to predict his moves when he had the ball in his hands, it was just as hard off the court.

After Kobe's devastating Achilles tendon injury, reporters expected him to respond with rage. Instead, his mood was philosophical. "You have to understand the fact that we're human," he said, putting aside his brashness. When other injuries dimmed the spotlight on his career, and he knew it was coming to an end, he wrote, "This isn't a death to me so much as it is an evolution, a transformation, or as Joseph Campbell would say, 'the new normal.'" If reporters had to scurry to discover that Campbell was the mythologist and author of *The Hero's Journey*, so be it. Kobe was happy to provide the tip. He didn't have much patience for empty clichés and superficial conversations. He preferred to go deep.

He had a daring side, too. While the classic video of him jumping over a speeding Aston Martin was done using special effects, it was true that he was drawn to motor sports and other fast things. He was often seen speeding through L.A. in one of his many vehicles, whether it was a Lamborghini, Range Rover, Escalade, Bentley Coupe, or motorcycle.

At the same time, Kobe was obsessed with Disneyland, which was only about 20 miles from his home in Newport Beach, California. He was known as one of the most frequent celebrity guests, visiting so often that he came to know many of the employees there. When Kobe started Granity Studios, he studied the history of the Walt Disney company. The way he talked about how "Walt" did his hiring and executed his vision made it seem like the Disney founder was an old friend. When the theme park celebrated the Lakers' 2009 championship with a parade, nobody else on the team but Kobe showed up, but he didn't mind. As he whooped it up on a parade float with Mickey Mouse, he was exuberant.

HAVE FAITH IN YOUR IDEAS

In his work, he was often unconventional. You could see it in his signature sneakers. In an unusual move early in his career he

SPEED DEMON

Kobe liked to zoom past gawking freeway commuters in his $300,000-plus Ferrari at high speeds. One reporter who accompanied him was so happy to reach the practice facility in one piece that, upon arrival, he said he felt like kissing the ground.

"I TRUST
THE TEAM.
I JUST
TRUST MYSELF
MORE."

SKY'S THE LIMIT

When Kobe was 21, he was among only five players to vote against the NBA players union's collective bargaining agreement that capped player salaries. Though he was barely even a starter at the time, he was thinking big and didn't want to limit future earnings.

paid $8 million to void his original shoe contract with Adidas and spent a year with no shoe deal. Many people considered the move crazy, but he was unhappy with the Adidas Kobe 2 shoe, which shoe experts later called the worst signature sneaker in history. Driven by his vision for the perfect basketball shoe, he eventually landed with Nike, where he obsessed over materials, balance, weight, traction, and durability. "My sneakers didn't just have to be comfortable," he explained, "they had to help me perform better."

Kobe had long been intrigued by how soccer players' movements could be so quick and sharp in low-cut shoes. In 2008, he asked Nike to produce a low-cut basketball sneaker, but there was strong resistance to the idea. The hoop world had forever embraced the concept that high-tops and mid-tops were mandatory for ankle protection. He challenged that conventional wisdom, called it a fallacy, and pushed hard until Nike created what he wanted. When the Kobe IV was released, it looked nothing like what basketball players had ever considered a serious shoe, and was the lowest-cut basketball shoe Nike had ever made. Many players loved them, including Kobe, who sported a pair as the Lakers won the title in 2009. A decade later, the popular, once-revolutionary Kobe IV would be worn by many NBA players, some of them the biggest names in the game, including Giannis Antetokounmpo, Luka Doncic, and Anthony Davis.

His role at Nike was also groundbreaking in another way—it made him a superstar in Asia. He was among the first players to take annual promotional treks to China, and he became an immensely well-liked figure in that enormous market, with hundreds of millions of fans. When he went to Beijing as part of the U.S. team at the 2008 Summer Olympics, he was among the biggest stars at the Games.

His eagerness to connect in foreign countries wasn't the norm among NBA players, but it helped make him an international icon. He credited his childhood spent in Europe, where so many distinct cultures are close by. "You kind of grow up with the understanding of adapting to other cultures and being curious about different cultures—the history, philosophy, the foods," he said. Chinese fans appreciated this attitude. "I think me having that openness and curiosity about their culture endeared me."

STICK OUT FROM THE CROWD

Kobe went against the grain. In establishing Granity Studios at the end of his hoop career, he didn't want his company to conform to what was trendy. He wanted to be part of the entertainment industry, but he also wanted to change it.

"I DON'T WANT TO BE THE NEXT MICHAEL JORDAN. I ONLY WANT TO BE KOBE BRYANT."

He had noticed that a lot of media content, especially when it was geared toward kids, was sloppily created. His brash goal was not to follow the trend, but to help raise the bar to a higher standard. "What we want to do," he said, unfolding his lofty vision, "is create stories that have been cared for, animation and scripts and lighting and performances that have been worked and reworked, and worked and reworked. These things need to be obsessed over, because I think that's what's missing in the world."

He absorbed the lessons of the top media experts he consulted and used what he learned to develop his own approach. He noticed that nobody was mixing sports and fantasy into the same stories, and he saw an opportunity there. But he didn't want to produce sweet little tales where everybody plays nice and wins. He envisioned something that would be true to his own experience. His idea was to show young people what it really takes to succeed in the world. His ESPN children's show, *Inside Kobe Bryant's Musecage,* used puppets to reflect on themes such as sacrifice and hard work, and explore how anger and other dark emotions can be used as motivation and provide a powerful source of energy. While his own celebrity brought the company attention, the unique and short-lived series sent a signal that Granity aimed to be different.

"WHEN I STEP ON THE COURT
I BECOME THAT.
I AM THE KILLER SNAKE."

"WHEN I'M IN THE CAGE, DON'T [*expletive*] TOUCH ME, DON'T TALK TO ME. JUST LEAVE ME ALONE."

DO THE UNEXPECTED

Nothing conveyed Kobe's sense of individualism more than his choice to change the numbers on his back. He spent the first 10 years of his career winning three titles while wearing number 8, before famously switching to his old youth-basketball number, 24, and winning two more championships. The new number had another meaning, too, since it reminded him of his 24-hour dedication to hoops. He ultimately became the first pro athlete to have two numbers retired by the same franchise.

It's rare for a superstar to change his jersey number midcareer, but it shouldn't have been surprising. Kobe was forever reinventing himself. He had arrived at the Lakers thinking he would be the top star, but quickly adjusted his vision and played the part of Shaq's young sidekick before ultimately becoming the face of the franchise. This wasn't the only case of Kobe evolving. Early in his career, he had adopted a clean-cut image off the court in order to appeal to corporate sponsors. Unlike many of his peers, he didn't have tattoos, he smiled often, and he

"I'M NOT SAD ABOUT IT. I'M VERY APPRECIATIVE OF WHAT I'VE HAD."

wore stylish suits. Looking back, he admitted this persona was modeled after other stars like Julius Erving and Michael Jordan. He would have to dig a little deeper before finding something more authentic to him.

When he was 21, he released a rap song featuring Tyra Banks called "K.O.B.E." that he performed at all-star weekend. It was widely mocked as cringe-worthy, and Kobe later agreed. It was clear that Kobe was no rap star. He would eventually say that the only good thing to come from the experience was that he got to hang around music-video shoots,

which was how he met a 17-year-old background dancer named Vanessa Laine. Six months later, while she was still in high school, they were engaged. A year after that, they were married.

FIND YOUR INNER BEAST

Kobe came to realize that he didn't need to be a rap star or everybody's favorite commercial pitchman. He didn't even need to smile. On the court, he could just be a fierce version of himself. Serious. Obsessive. Intense. In time, this became his alter ego, and he became known throughout the world as the "Black Mamba."

He got the name from the 2003 movie *Kill Bill: Vol. 1*, in which "Black Mamba" was the code name for the assassin played by Uma Thurman. Kobe liked the sound of it, and did some research, discovering that it referred to a lethal African snake known for its speed and aggression. Soon after, he began calling himself the "Black Mamba."

The transformation would make him feel ruthless, indestructible, and ready to devour. "It's like an actor getting ready for a film," he explained when discussing how the Black Mamba mentality got him in the right head space. "You've got to put yourself in that cage. When you're in the cage you are the character, and when you leave there, it's something completely different."

KEEP IT REAL

For most of his career, the Mamba raged and was one of the most celebrated athletes of his generation. Late in his career, after squeezing everything he could out of his body, he began noticing the inevitable decline that every athlete endures. Those who knew him thought he'd be devastated to give up the game and might fool himself into staying too long. But Kobe didn't do delusions. Ever realistic, he surprised many observers and accepted aging with grace. "It's the natural progression of growth, of maturation. I mean, there's no sadness in that ... I see the beauty in not being able to blow past defenders anymore, you know what I mean?"

Of course, if anyone thought he would go out meekly, they didn't know him. In that final game, he overcame exhaustion and a beat-up body to launch 50 shots and 12 free throws. It wasn't always pretty. But, in the end, he somehow found the magic one more time, thrilling the crowd for one more unforgettable feat. All this was punctuated by the final declaration in his goodbye speech after the game, as he dropped the mic at center court and declared "Mamba out!" The moment was so instantly iconic that two weeks later, the president

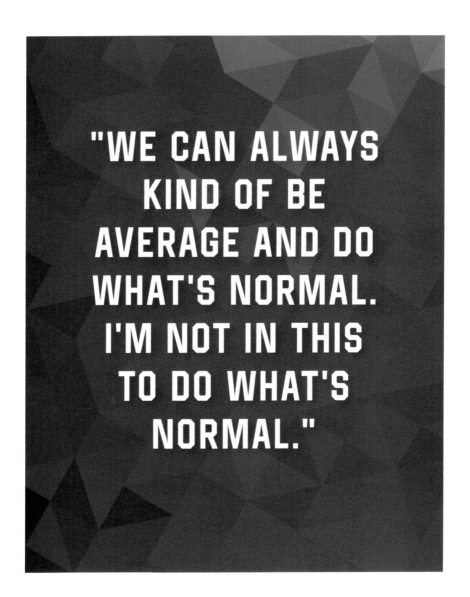

"WE CAN ALWAYS KIND OF BE AVERAGE AND DO WHAT'S NORMAL. I'M NOT IN THIS TO DO WHAT'S NORMAL."

of the United States stole the line to use at the end of his final White House Correspondents' Dinner speech, proclaiming "Obama out."

Then Kobe just turned the page. He became part of a venture capital group that went on a winning streak, investing in companies that included the hugely successful Body Armor sports drink and the innovative internet smash LegalZoom. All the while, he was developing Granity Studios. Although he had enough money and free time to sit back and play golf, that wouldn't be him.

Eight months after his final game, his third daughter was born. Someone mentioned that as she grew up, she would likely know him more as a creator and producer than as a basketball player. Buoyed by his belief in the power of reinvention, he didn't seem to mind that idea at all. "She won't know that part of my life, but that doesn't bother me at all," he said. "In fact, it excites me.

LESSONS FROM A LEGEND

- **TRUST YOURSELF.**
- **LOVE WHAT YOU LOVE, WITHOUT APOLOGY.**
- **STAND OUT FROM THE REST.**
- **DON'T CONFORM. KEEP THEM GUESSING.**

KEEP COMING BACK

From a distance, Kobe's life looked almost flawless. An exotic Italian boyhood. High school stardom. The good fortune to land with the sport's most successful franchise. A beautiful family and long career. But get closer and you see the struggles and the setbacks. No doubt, his successes outweighed his failures, but along the way there were problems. To get where he ended up, he needed resilience, redemption, and the ability to rise from the depths and come back strong.

Even on the court he struggled with setbacks. Playing the youth circuit in Italy, he dominated. But at the age of 12, he spent the summer in the U. S. playing against the tougher competition of Philadelphia's prestigious Sonny Hill League, where he was completely overmatched. He was suffering with Osgood-Schlatter disease, a chronic knee inflammation that plagued him in his teens. Even touching his knees was excruciating. "The league was probably 25 games, and I didn't score a basket, a free throw, nothing," he recalled. "At the end, I sobbed my eyes out."

For the next year, he lived with his family in France where his dad was playing professionally. The summer league experience provided major motivation. He practiced almost nonstop, determined to score at least two points the following summer. It became his mantra: *One basket. One basket!* When he returned to Philly the next summer, he scored far more than two points, and captured the attention of scouts. After that, he could envision a future in basketball. He had learned the importance of working through a setback. It was a simple lesson, but it stuck, and never left him.

When he was a freshman in high school, his team was dreadful, losing 17 times in 21 games. That kind of embarrassment was unacceptable to him, so he worked on his game at all hours to try to change it. By the time he was a senior, the team was 31-3, with Kobe averaging 31 points, 12 rebounds, seven assists, four blocks, and four steals a game while playing all five positions.

It was this dominating level of performance that got him noticed by the Sixers. When they invited him to scrimmage with the pros, he would often be knocked around hard, as the older players took some pleasure in introducing the upstart kid to the rough, physical style that defined the NBA of the 1990s. Joe Bryant recalled big, burly Rick Mahorn using his wide body to set a hard screen on Kobe, flooring the scrawny teenager. When his son popped up and kept playing, his dad knew he had passed a test. It was a

"I FIGURED OUT IF YOU KEEP PUSHING, YOU'LL KEEP GETTING BETTER."

sign that he could bounce back from the hard NBA knocks yet to come.

KEEP YOUR CHIN UP

In his first season, the biggest blow came in the final moments. It was 1997 and Kobe was playing in the fifth game of a hard-fought playoff series that the mighty Utah Jazz led 3-1. It was the first chance for Laker fans and the rest of the basketball world to see their young phenom in a big-pressure situation. It didn't go well. In fact, it became one of the most embarrassing playoff performances in NBA history.

In front of a raucous Utah crowd, the 18-year-old got the ball in the final seconds of a tie game and darted to the right elbow of the key, where he took a fairly easy 15-footer to try to win it at the buzzer. It fell way short. In the season's biggest moment, he had delivered the most humiliating play in basketball—an air ball. This sent the game into overtime, where almost immediately, the defense left him completely alone to launch a 3-pointer. Again, way short. Air ball. The crowd roared.

With 43 seconds left in OT, he got another chance, a 3-pointer from beyond the top of the key. Again, way short. Air ball. At this point the crowd was almost delirious. But the game remained close and the Lakers were still alive, down three points with seven seconds to go. If they win, they extend the series. If they lose, they go home for the summer. Kobe launched a 3-pointer to try to tie the game. For the fourth time, way short. Air ball.

The highly touted first-round choice that the Lakers had traded for suddenly looked like a bust. He hadn't just come up small in an elimination game. His performance in the clutch had been historically terrible. The biggest shots he had ever taken didn't even reach the rim. What was most telling, though, was not the failure itself, but how he reacted.

As the game ended, Shaq tried to console him, but Kobe assured him that it wasn't needed. "Somebody had to take the shots, and I was going to take them," he said later.

"WHEN THE GAME IS MORE IMPORTANT THAN THE INJURY ITSELF, YOU DON'T FEEL THAT DAMN INJURY."

"I wouldn't have it any other way. If I made them, I would have been the hero." If he was crushed that night, he didn't show it. Ever confident, he walked off with his chin up.

When the plane landed in L.A., he went to Palisades High School and shot the ball all night and into the morning. The next day he went back and did it again. While the whole basketball world was abuzz over his epic fail, he was trying to figure out what went wrong. He didn't think he had choked under the pressure. There was nothing wrong with his shooting form on the four shots,

and he had never been the nervous type. He quickly realized that what caused his debacle wasn't in his head, but in his body. He was too exhausted to make those shots, and his legs were too weak—they had felt "like spaghetti." He knew he had to get stronger.

The game in Utah was the 80th game he had played that season. The previous year, back in high school in Pennsylvania, he had played 34 games. The physical demands of his first NBA season had taken its toll. If he wanted to come back from this disaster, he was going to have to find more endurance. "You're walking around and it's embarrassing because you shot the air balls," he later said. But he found his way through it by turning it into a challenge he could meet: "I looked at it with rationality. The reason I shot air balls was because my legs weren't there. Next year, they'll be there." Now he was especially glad that he had turned down Spike Lee's movie-role offer for that summer. He had something specific to work on.

Despite the humiliation, or maybe because of it, missing those four shots did lead to enormous accomplishments for Kobe. The next year, he came back noticeably stronger. Stamina became his obsession, and remained a focus for the rest of his career. His trainer tailored an intense workout program to prepare him for the long season and postseason. Over the course of his career, Kobe became renowned for his otherworldly endurance and late-game heroics, especially in the playoffs when other players were faltering from the cumulative exhaustion

of a long season. In all, he made 15 postseason runs with the Lakers, winning 33 of 43 series. He never got caught being too tired again.

STAY IN THE GAME

Kobe's pro career began with a bad break—literally. After being drafted but before his first training camp, he fell hard and broke his left wrist while playing pickup basketball at Venice Beach. The recovery took him six weeks and cost him most of that first camp, and the physical obstacles only got worse after that. Throughout his career, he lost games to various arm and hand injuries— fingers that were lacerated or badly broken, a fractured metacarpal bone in his hand, a sprained shoulder. His legs fared even worse, with chronic knee swelling and soreness, severely sprained ankles on multiple occasions, sore feet, bruised shin, various forms of tendonitis. And these were just the minor injuries.

To be a professional athlete is to play with pain. In his final seasons, he knew the price well. "As you get older, your body starts breaking down and you really have to love the process in order to get through that," he said in his 19th season. "Like, right now, I hurt. My ankle joints, my knee joints. My back. My thighs are sore." But Kobe kept playing on. It's one of the main reasons he could never understand Shaq, who would be sidelined for weeks by a toe injury.

For Kobe, the right response to routine injuries was to put mind over matter and get back to getting the job done. No excuses. To illustrate his point, he would use the example of someone taking time off on the couch because of a pulled hamstring. That person may claim that they can barely move, but, Kobe said, if the house caught fire, suddenly they would be moving. They would be off that couch and bounding upstairs to do whatever it takes to get their family to safety. "The reason is that the lives of your family are more important than the injury of your hamstring," he said. If it meant enough to you, Kobe believed, you'd rally.

SHAKE IT OFF

Setbacks, Kobe knew, were a chance to shine. The lows could be followed by incredible highs, so it was best to see it through. In 1999, for example, he missed two crucial free throws to cost the Lakers a key playoff game against San Antonio. But the misses were forgotten when the Lakers won championships the next three seasons.

Of course, these kinds of turnarounds didn't come easy, and required Kobe to maintain unwavering confidence in himself. He knew how to do that. He knew that you couldn't retreat when things didn't go well. If you were a scorer in a slump, by Kobe's rules, you could still take 30 shots in the next game even if you missed them all. What you couldn't do was question your abilities and take significantly fewer shots. If you do that, you've beaten yourself. That was the essence of the Kobe philosophy: Keep firing. Keep working. "I have moments and I have days where I doubt myself," he said. "But to me, that's the exciting

"HATERS ARE A
GOOD PROBLEM
TO HAVE. NOBODY
HATES THE GOOD
ONES. THEY HATE
THE GREAT ONES."

"SOMETIMES YOU PUSH SO HARD THAT YOU BREAK. BUT THEN WHEN YOU BREAK YOU SEE WHAT YOU'RE MADE OF."

part of the challenge." Kobe felt that hitting a slump could be good for an athlete: "[It's] a great opportunity to come out and show everybody this is how you bounce back. This is how your respond to a challenge."

He would use a failure as motivation to come back stronger than before, and put in countless hours to make sure it wouldn't happen again. After losing the finals to Boston in 2008, he once again doubled down on his endurance training with smart, intense workouts. With his trainer Tim Grover, he fashioned a regimen that specifically strengthened areas that had been susceptible to

injury, such as his ankles, wrists, and hips. This was especially important because, in addition to the long playoff runs that the Lakers were enduring almost every year, he also had another huge new responsibility: His country was now counting on him to play in the 2008 Beijing Olympics.

Being named captain of that year's Olympic "Redeem Team" was perhaps the greatest honor of Kobe's life. The team would be tasked with reclaiming the gold medal after the U.S. team fell short in 2004. His participation would test his body in a big way—he, like most

NBA players, used the summer to rest and recover from the demands of the season. The Olympics took place in the summer, so there would be no such luxury for Kobe or his Olympic teammates. The schedule was packed with practices and games, and little meaningful rest for months and years on end. He would need all the endurance and injury prevention he could muster.

The sweat was worth it. Despite all the extra mileage, his body stayed strong. For years, nagging injuries had threatened to diminish him, but finally now, for this key era of his career, he wasn't reliant on ankle braces, shoulder wraps, and sleeves. He had worked fiercely and made himself whole. In Beijing, in a hard-fought gold-medal game against Spain, he scored 20 points, including 13 in the final eight minutes, to lead the U.S. to gold. His day job was going well, too. In each of the next two summers, the Lakers enjoyed jubilant victory parades in Los Angeles. Then, in 2012, as a key contributor to the U.S. team, he won gold again.

LEARN TO REBOUND

Late in his career, his seasons were defined by getting hurt, not winning titles. He got through his final year unscathed, but various injuries ended the three previous seasons. First came the ruptured Achilles in April 2013. It was expected to sideline him for at least a year. Remarkably, just eight months later, he was back on the court, though he looked stiff and not quite the same athlete he had been before. In his sixth game after returning, as he launched into a spin move, he twisted his leg awkwardly and fell to the floor. The diagnosis was a fractured bone in his left knee,

---

STAT ⚡ Kobe missed 14,481 shots from the field, more than any other player in NBA history, and a thousand more misses than the next closest player.

---

and another finished season. The next year, rotator cuff surgery was the culprit, costing him the last 38 games of the season.

He saw these as disappointments but also as tests. Whatever the injury, his goal was to come back stronger. This meant taking on recovery with his typical unrelenting style. The night of the Achilles injury, his first thought was that maybe he had just played his last game. He was already an older player, finishing his 17th year. He understood the severity of the injury; the comeback would be arduous and even if it went well, he might never move with the same speed and fluidity. As these thoughts began swirling in his head, his wife and daughters came into the training room. They were devastated and worried, and the family cried together.

He told his kids that Daddy would be OK. And at that moment, he knew he wasn't done. He didn't want his kids to see him limp off as his final act. He would be back. "The Achilles injury was my personal Mount Everest," he said later. He was fueled by a determination to conquer it:

"People were saying I might not be able to come back, but I knew I was not going to let it beat me. I was not going to let an injury dictate my retirement. I was going to dictate my retirement. That's when I decided I had to climb that mountain."

Before he left the arena, he and his doctors scheduled his surgery for the following morning. No time to waste.

ENDURE THE LOWS

The biggest crisis of Kobe's life wasn't a basketball injury, but something much worse. In July 2003, when he was 24 and had been married for three years, with a 6-month-old baby at home, he traveled to Colorado to undergo relatively minor knee surgery. Upon checking into a sprawling, castle-like lodge on a hillside about 40 minutes from Vail, he was given a brief tour of the property by the 19-year-old female front desk clerk. The woman later told authorities that the tour ended in his room, where the two consensually kissed.

What exactly happened after that was discussed worldwide, but was never proven or disproven in court. The woman's initial account stated that when she attempted to leave the room Kobe stopped her and committed a sexual assault. He admitted to having sex with the woman, but insisted she consented. A couple of weeks later, he was charged with felony sexual assault.

When Kobe was charged, everything changed almost instantly. He was facing 25 years to life in prison. Out on bail when the season began, he would regularly fly to Colorado for legal proceedings, spend the day in court, fly back to L.A., and play a game the same night. He did this more than a dozen times, and the physical and mental toll left him drained.

At home, things were awful. Vanessa was livid, but Kobe begged her not to leave him. As he later recounted to ESPN's Ramona Shelburne, after one big argument he found all his clothes thrown into the street. He played that night and scored only one point in the first half; he was so distraught, scared, and humiliated by the mistakes he had made. With his life spiraling downward, he clung to what he

"EVERYTHING NEGATIVE— PRESSURE, CHALLENGES— IS ALL AN OPPORTUNITY FOR ME TO RISE."

knew best. "I remember sitting in the locker room at halftime and saying to myself, 'You know what, you may lose everything in life because of the situation you put yourself in. You may lose your family, your freedom, but I'll be damned if I lose basketball, because this [expletive] I can control.'" He had always used his work as an outlet for deep emotions, a way to express what was otherwise bottled inside. In this case, rage, fear, and frustration were his fuel. That night, he scored 24 points in the fourth quarter, was a fierce defender, and led the Lakers to an overtime win. After the game, though, he went to a hotel for the night, alone. It felt like rock bottom.

For 14 months, his fate hung in the balance. But just before his trial was to begin, the accuser decided not to testify and charges were dropped. At that point, in a rare move for a high-profile defendant in such a case, he apologized for his behavior and the pain the incident had caused her. He said he had come to understand her point of view that consent wasn't granted, even though he saw the situation differently and did not admit guilt.

"I WILL NOT MAKE THE SAME MISTAKES IN THE FUTURE THAT I HAVE MADE IN THE PAST. I WILL MAKE NEW MISTAKES, I AM SURE."

Six months later, the two settled a civil case for an undisclosed sum, and both agreed to not publicly comment on it again.

LET IT GO

In time, his marriage healed. He apologized to Vanessa profusely and publicly. But his reputation was shattered. Almost all of his sponsors dropped him. His jersey sales plunged. He was excoriated by women's rights advocates. In the perception of many, he had gone from hero to villain overnight.

He sought out a priest, who told him to let it go, that other people's reactions were not within his control. That conversation proved to be a turning point. He had always hated the phoniness of being famous—of having to live up to some bland, idealized media creation of who he was supposed to be. Now, in a strange way, after this public fall, he felt like he had nothing to lose. He was free to be himself. "That's when I decided that if people were going to like me or not like me, it was going to be for who I actually was," he said. "To hell with all that plain vanilla [expletive], just to get endorsement deals. Those are superficial, anyway."

This transformation took many forms. He fired the agent who had been with him since he was 17 and replaced him with a new agent, Rob Pelinka, who would be one of his closest associates for the rest of his life. It was around this time that he got his first tattoos (including one devoted to Vanessa) and adopted the Black Mamba alter ego. Nike, the only major sponsor to stick with him, released a snake logo and signature Mamba sneaker. In a move inspired by his daughters, he became a major advocate for women's basketball, promoting the WNBA and working closely with female collegiate basketball stars. Reporters and teammates started noticing that Kobe, once known for his arrogance, seemed a bit humbled by his fall. Over time, he came across as nicer, friendlier, and happier. Having survived such a harrowing year, he seemed renewed.

> ## "ONCE YOU KNOW WHAT FAILURE FEELS LIKE, DETERMINATION CHASES SUCCESS."

About six weeks before the charges were dropped, Shaq was traded away. The Lakers became Kobe's team, and as always, he worked intensely to make them champions again. Many people in the basketball world came to admire his comeback. "He took that negative and turned it into a positive," Michael Jordan said about Kobe. "He changed his life. He continued to dedicate himself to the game and made sure that one incident would not define him."

MAKE IT THROUGH

Kobe valued resilience and strived for it. Like all of us, he had ongoing struggles. Even after significantly repairing his reputation, his personal issues lingered. Eight years after the Colorado incident, Vanessa filed for divorce. He knew his intense personality was difficult to live with, but saving his marriage became his new obsession. He fought hard for his family. "My reputation as an athlete is that I'm extremely determined, and that I will work my ass off," he said. "How could I do that in my professional life if I wasn't like that in my personal life, when it affects my kids?" After more than a year of separation, the couple was able to reconcile.

In the years after retiring, there was less pressure and less travel. Kobe had more time to spend at home. People who knew him said that his marriage was solid after retirement; that he never seemed more content. He was still working hard building his new career, but he also had room for simpler goals. Ever competitive, he made a point to be first every day in the school parking lot pickup line. He and Vanessa not only saved their family, but grew it, welcoming their third and fourth daughters, Bianka and Capri, in 2016 and 2019, respectively.

Kobe was proud of his perseverance. As a player, he had always said games were more fun when the Lakers fell behind. It would force him to find a way to win. In that huge game seven of the 2010 finals against Boston, his shots weren't falling and the team was way behind, but he didn't panic. He pulled down 15 rebounds, a remarkable number for a guard, and scored key baskets with the game on the line. That night he missed 18 of 24 shots. In fact, overall in his career, he missed more shots than anyone ever, but he didn't care. The Lakers won, and the misses only made him stronger.

LESSONS FROM A LEGEND

- 🏀 WHEN YOU FALL OR GET KNOCKED DOWN, GET UP.
- 🏀 DON'T PITY YOURSELF. SOLVE THE PROBLEM AND IMPROVE.
- 🏀 MAKE RESILIENCE ONE OF YOUR CORE QUALITIES.

LEAVE A LEGACY

CHAPTER 8

In Kobe's version of a well-lived life, you dream big, plan well, and work hard. You find meaning, immersing yourself in something that matters to you, learning and improving as you go and overcoming the obstacles that inevitably come your way. You discover your own personal sense of peace and purpose, and don't worry much about what other people think of you. And then, you pass it along to the next generation.

The irony is that, while Kobe was known for his ego, he spent a lot time thinking about how to share his experiences and insight with other people. "I enjoy passing things on," he said around the time of his retirement. "If we're not helping the world move forward, what are we doing?" This is why he mentored so many young players, and why he created a company that uses stories to convey valuable perspectives about sports and life.

The idea of a legacy intrigued him. He might not have cared what critics or naysayers thought in the short term, but he did care about the overall impact of his life. He contemplated big questions. What was he achieving with all this hard work? How would he be remembered? What could he learn and share? What lives would be touched by his work? It was important to leave the right mark.

EARN YOUR PLACE

On the court, Kobe's legend is secure. He scored more points than any guard who ever played, even Jordan. He reached 40 points 134 times. He scored 50 points 26 times, and, in one stretch, did it four games in a row. He was so accomplished that the Lakers said both of his jersey numbers would have been retired individually even if the other half of his career didn't exist. Fans won't soon forget his signature blend of intensity and skill. The completeness of his game. The 135 playoff wins. The two gold medals. The 6,286 assists that no one ever talks about (second all-time among shooting guards.) The clutch game-winners from deep. The Mamba mentality.

Those who saw his career up-close knew it was special. "He was the most intelligent professional athlete I had ever encountered," wrote longtime NBA reporter Jackie MacMullan. "[He was] curious and demanding and savvy and competitive and relentless and infinitely complicated." She pointed out that his fierceness was, at times, so strong that it unsettled his peers. Another longtime NBA writer, Chris Ballard, noted that

"YOU HAVE TO WORK HARD
IN THE DARK TO
SHINE IN THE LIGHT."

few athletes have ever seemed more invincible or purposeful, and that whatever Kobe did, from hitting a jump shot to raising daughters, his goal was simple and powerful: Do it better than anyone ever has.

For a whole generation of players, his example was a template. At his last all-star game, even though his skills had diminished with age and injury, he got more all-star votes from the fans than any other player. In a league full of superstars, he was the people's choice. That weekend, NBA luminaries, including Carmelo Anthony, Dwyane Wade, and Chris Paul, took him to dinner and each person around the table told Kobe what he meant to them. An observer later noted the similarity of each speech. They all said that when they started in the NBA, their first big goal was to earn his respect.

GO FOR GREATNESS

In his retirement years, a steady stream of NBA stars sought out Kobe for advice, including Anthony Davis, LeBron James, and Kevin Durant. LeBron was especially grateful, saying that Kobe's success had provided the inspiration he needed to also go directly from high school to the pros. Inevitably, they all got a similar message from their mentor: Don't accept being good; do whatever possible to be great.

Kobe's intensity was felt by many future NBA players around the world. Jayson Tatum, from St. Louis, and Joel Embiid, from Cameroon, both said that they started playing basketball because they wanted to be like Kobe. Spencer Dinwiddie, from South Central L.A., said, "He was everything to a lot of kids. And I was one of them." Growing up in Greece, Giannis Antetokounmpo tried to learn all he could from Kobe's game. He said most of the young players he knew in Europe did the same. In Kobe's final season, the two met on the court and Kobe told the budding star that he had the ability and intelligence to achieve greatness, but it wasn't enough. He needed to work harder than everyone else. He publicly challenged Antetokounmpo to win

> STAT ⚡ **Bryant scored more than 60 points in a game six times over the course of his career. The only other player in league history to do this was Wilt Chamberlain.**

an MVP award. When he did win it in 2019, Kobe set his sights higher, immediately challenging him to win a championship ring.

WNBA players got similar instructions. Marina Mabrey met him when she joined the L.A. Sparks and later described him as a father figure. He would reach out to her at games or by text, and stress the importance of studying the game and never losing confidence, always reminding her that just being good enough isn't good enough. Another Sparks player, Chelsea Gray, called him one of the best human beings she ever met. He and Gianna would spend time around the team, because he wanted his daughter to see pro women players as role models. When Gray worked out with Kobe, he didn't toss empty compliments at her. Instead, he truly tried to

help, focusing his advice on the moves she needed when everything was on the line and defenders were playing aggressively.

Chris Webber said Kobe changed the league by making NBA players more serious. They had to be fully engaged to play against him, and many adopted a tough, no-nonsense approach to be like him. His career convinced a generation of players that unrelenting effort was the vehicle to success. One such player was Steph Curry, who said the most important Mamba lesson he learned was about showing up every day with fire, competitiveness, and a focus on championships.

But Kobe wasn't just a hard-edged mentor. He had a softer side, often reaching out to players when times were toughest. After the WNBA's reigning MVP Breanna Stewart ruptured her Achilles tendon in 2019, he immediately texted his support. NBA player Draymond Green remembered struggling during a conference final series and getting a motivational text from Kobe that said: "If making history was easy, why bother?"

GIVE THEM SOMETHING TO REMEMBER

The day Kobe announced his retirement by posting his poem, "Dear Basketball," on The Players' Tribune, the site crashed. It should not have been a surprise to anyone. Kobe had made the passage from NBA star to cultural icon. He even influenced the language of the game and beyond. At some point, it became cool for kids and many

adults to yell his name for emphasis when taking a long shot in a pickup game, or just throwing a piece of trash into a can, or even lobbing a projectile successfully in a video game. In the past 20 years, it's become a common practice around the world. Kobe said he even did it sometimes when tossing something into his own trash basket. And NBA players can still be seen yelling it out on long jumpers. Nobody screams "Jordan" or "LeBron." They yell "Kobe!"

Celebrities of all kinds were Kobe fans. When Dustin Hoffman was caught on the Staples Center scoreboard kiss cam at the 2010 finals, it wasn't his wife he was caught kissing but a picture of

"THAT'S THE BEAUTY OF LIFE, YOU DON'T KNOW HOW IT IS GOING TO END."

Kobe. The crowd loved it. Hip-hop stars were no less enamored. He was such a major figure in urban culture, the references were countless. Lil Wayne had a 2009 hit with a song called "Kobe Bryant." Throughout his career and after, the biggest rap stars weaved him into their verses. In one song, Kanye West dreamed about playing him. Nicki Minaj fantasized about being him. Big Sean bragged about shooting more shots than him, Jay-Z rapped that he could shoot faster, while 50 Cent boasted that he could shoot a gun better than Kobe could shoot a three. Ice Cube memorialized him beating Boston in the finals. J. Cole bragged that he could ball like Kobe. Kendrick Lamar captured the drama of him in the clutch in this line from the song "Mona Lisa": "Four minute on the clock, Black Mamba with the ball."

After Kobe's tragic death in a helicopter crash in 2020, an outpouring of grief and love welled up from every corner of the planet. Los Angeles went into unprecedented mourning. Players and fans wept on NBA broadcasts. A couple in California created a 115-foot-tall Kobe mural in the grass of a baseball field. In the Philippines, just two days after Kobe died, a tenement basketball court was repainted with a mural of Kobe and 13-year-old Gianna, who was also killed in the crash. When the Lakers won the 2020 championship, their fans gathered at the Staples Center to celebrate,

"AS EASY AS GOD GIVES IT TO YOU, HE CAN TAKE IT AWAY."

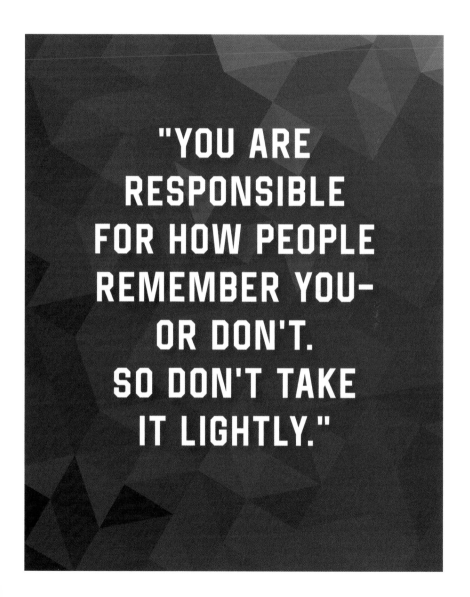

"YOU ARE RESPONSIBLE FOR HOW PEOPLE REMEMBER YOU– OR DON'T. SO DON'T TAKE IT LIGHTLY."

but it wasn't the names of the winning players the fans shouted. Seven months after the accident and more than four years since he had last suited up, they chanted Kobe's name. .

On the NASCAR racetrack, car No. 24 was painted purple and yellow in tribute. In the NFL, players wrote his name on their cleats, while NHL players wrote his name on their sticks. A pro tennis player wore a Kobe jersey during warm-ups at the Australian Open, while the world's No. 1 player, Novak Djokovic, spoke movingly about how Kobe had mentored him through a period of injury. Near the end of 2020, BabyCenter announced that the name "Gianna" had seen a spike in popularity on the list of most popular baby names of the year, ranking in the Top 25 overall. The fastest-rising boys name was Kobe.

DO GOOD

Throughout his life, Kobe Bryant contributed time and money to a wide variety of charities, including the work he did as the official spokesperson for the After-School All-Stars, a nonprofit that offers after-school programs to kids in 14 U.S. cities. He also partnered with a Chinese foundation to create the Kobe Bryant China Fund, providing cash for education and sports needs in China. He and his wife donated $1 million to the Call of Duty Endowment, which helps U.S. military veterans find careers. They were also among the founding donors of the National Museum of African American History and Culture in Washington, D.C., donating a million dollars. Kobe worked with cancer charities, and made more than 100 appearances for the Make-A-Wish Foundation over two decades of involvement. He hosted free basketball camps for the Boys & Girls Club of America, and was part of the NBA Cares initiatives, helping build homes and basketball courts, stocking food pantries, and supporting reading initiatives. He also was a spokesperson for Aid Still Required, a group that helps victims left behind after natural disasters and other crises.

In 2007, the Kobe and Vanessa Bryant Foundation was established and soon began sponsoring international enrichment experiences for minority college students while also working with other groups to combat homelessness. Some of Kobe's good works were spontaneous in nature; just a month before his death, he witnessed a major multivehicle accident at a foggy intersection near his home. Viral video caught him just after he jumped out of his SUV and took action, checking on victims and working to settle the scene until help arrived.

His decisions weren't always popular. In 2012, he was criticized for not supporting the social justice movement quickly enough. He didn't join other players who wore hoodies in protest of the shooting of Trayvon Martin that year. But as the movement grew, Kobe got more involved. Ultimately, he spoke at a rally with Martin's parents, and began more vigorously supporting causes to prevent wrongful deaths and unequal treatment of minorities, including appearing in ads for the Southern Poverty Law Center, a longtime leading civil rights organization.

In 2018, he called Colin Kaepernick the most impressive leader among all current Black athletes, lauding the bravery of the NFL star who was effectively blackballed for protesting racial inequality. He donated to Kaepernick's efforts to aid at-risk minority families and spoke publicly against those who assailed the quarterback. He acknowledged that as an athlete, there is often trepidation to jump into such controversies for fear of alienating some fans. But, Kobe said, when you feel moved to do the

"LEAVE EVERYTHING ON THE COURT. LEAVE THE GAME BETTER THAN YOU FOUND IT."

right thing, staying on the sidelines is not an option.

AIM TO INSPIRE

One of his goals in creating Granity Studios was to diversify the entertainment industry with an eye toward hiring more minorities and women, an objective that in 2019 he called his "next obsession." He had learned that the entertainment industry was severely lacking in diversity, especially in behind-the-scenes roles like animators and writers. He saw it as a challenge and wanted to be the person to change that. He believed fresh perspectives would lead to stories that could inspire the world in new ways. This meant hiring and training a more diverse set of animators and writers, and creating content with a wider representation of voices and characters.

In choosing stories and characters, Kobe always pressed for originality. If something felt too comfortable or familiar, he rejected it. The result was that Granity specialized in sports and fantasy projects that were far from typical. In the Wizenard book series he created, a mystical coach inspires his players with mind-opening drills, such as making them watch a flower grow or having them figure out how to retrieve a ball guarded by a tiger. Across content and formats, the company's goal was to show kids that magic is within them and all around them.

Michael Jackson had impressed upon Kobe the importance of leaving behind "something timeless." Kobe knew that Granity was one of the ways he could make this happen. He was insistent on creating fun tales, full of joy and imagination, with important truths tucked inside. "We teach them compassion and empathy, work ethic and attention to detail," he said, referring to the impact Granity projects had on kids. In each adventure, he aimed to give young readers something tangible they could use in their own lives, highlighting themes like self-acceptance and growth, and showing kids how to solve internal and external conflicts.

Kobe had dreamed up the details of a fictional dreamscape during his final Lakers training camp in Hawaii, and it had helped form the basis for his new company. He jotted down extensive notes and developed an intricate backstory describing a magical universe and all the kingdoms and rules within it. He called it "Granity," a shortened form of "greater than infinity," because

"INSPIRE ONE WHO INSPIRES THE NEXT WHO INSPIRES THE NEXT AND ON AND ON YOU GO. AND THAT'S THE FOUNDATION OF IT ALL."

he wanted to motivate generations of young readers to think big. His goal was to make things that would last. "The fundamental belief of the company is to create forever," he explained in 2019. "That's how you create something that's greater than infinity."

The night that Granity's animated film, "Dear Basketball," won the Oscar for Best Animated Short Film, he admitted this validation in a new field felt better than winning an NBA title. On the stage for his acceptance speech, he took a dig at television pundit Laura Ingraham, who had suggested that basketball players should just "shut up and dribble." He had no intention of doing that. Instead, he boldly proclaimed, "I'm going to do something in this next 20 years that is better than these last 20."

MAKE TODAY COUNT

Kobe remains revered by millions for more than his good works and

"KNOW THIS ABOVE ALL ELSE. FULLY USE EVERY POINT, MOMENT, AND HOUR THAT YOU HAVE. TIME WAITS FOR NO MAN. SEIZE THE DAY."

short storytelling career; he's remembered for the inspiring example he set. He knew that this was the essence of his appeal— the alchemy of his thrilling natural ability combined with his old-fashioned work ethic. "I felt extremely blessed by God-given talent," he said. "But at the same time, I didn't take it for granted at all. I think that's a very powerful message to have." And it was powerful. Powerful enough to create a lasting legacy.

Because of his intense attention to detail, Kobe was often called a perfectionist. But that characterization doesn't quite capture it. Perfection wasn't the goal he was after. He got satisfaction not from tidy end results but from fully engaging his talent day after day in challenges that he considered worthwhile. That was his everything.

As he recovered from his Achilles surgery, he became obsessed with Achilles himself, the mythic Greek hero who chose a short life of consequence and glory over a long,

peaceful life that is uneventful and soon forgotten. It's no wonder that Kobe felt drawn to him. It wasn't because Kobe wanted a short life. He didn't. But he was intent on living his life with passion and purpose, as if it *might* end at any time.

VALUE LOYALTY

After his retirement, when NBA players started taking off games just for rest, Kobe was incredulous. He imagined the fan who pays hundreds of dollars showing up at the arena only to find out his favorite player is taking the night off. He could never have done that to his fans. In this way, and many others, he was among the last of the old-school athletes. Unlike most players who jump from team to team for more money or to join other stars for a better chance to win, Kobe stayed put.

In his last two seasons, L.A.'s record was the second worst in the NBA, and Lakers owner Jeanie Buss told him that she hated to see such a great player end his career on a hapless team. She offered to

"I'M AT THE GYM AT THE SAME TIME AFTER LOSING 50 GAMES AS I AM AFTER WINNING A CHAMPIONSHIP. IT DOESN'T CHANGE FOR ME."

trade him to a contender, but he refused. "Just because the ship is sinking," he noted, "you can't all of a sudden just say, 'I'm going to go jump off and swim to another ship.'" He went on to explain: "If you can win championships in front of everybody, then you can miss the playoffs in front of everybody. You've got to be able to take both sides of it."

STAY CONSISTENT, KEEP IMPROVING

Kobe's 81-point game is often considered his masterpiece.

But in Kobe's eyes, his greatest achievement was never going to be one game, series, or even a shelf full of awards and rings. He was interested in leaving behind something bigger, a body of work, a model of excellence. In his mind, the masterpiece was the whole thing—the process, the approach, the highs he reached, the struggles he overcame, and the impact it all had.

For him, consistency mattered. Improvement was lifeblood. In game 7 of the conference finals against Portland in 2000, the Lakers were in deep trouble before roaring back for a victory, punctuated by a late alley-oop from Kobe to Shaq, an exhilarating play that became one of the most memorable of their careers. The team went on to win the title, but Kobe wasn't fully satisfied. He was bothered by his own performance and how close they had come to losing. The Trail Blazers had used big guards to repeatedly post him up. It wore him out and affected his scoring. He recognized that he needed to get stronger. So rather than bask in the championship glow, he got to work, and in the offseason added 20 pounds and a layer of muscle. The fans focused on the alley-oop. But Kobe focused on equipping himself for the battles to come. That's where he always went—back to work.

LEAD BY EXAMPLE

One major reason Kobe stayed so dedicated was that he wanted to be a good role model for his four daughters. As he got older, he was eager to overcome the actions that had embarrassed him and sullied his reputation as a younger man. His adult relationship with his own parents was rocky, including long periods of estrangement. Kobe said they hadn't supported his marriage and later tried to cash in on his fame by selling his memorabilia without his consent. But whatever the issues, he put his focus on his own wife and kids and became a proud family man.

He boasted often about the joys of being a girl dad, joking that he would love to have five more girls. Family games of "tickle man" became a favorite pastime, and his predawn and midnight workouts were purposely scheduled for when the kids were sleeping, so he could spend more time with them when they were awake.

In his playing days, he would sometimes fly home after a road game to be there for a birthday celebration, and then fly back to join the team the next day, playing games on little or no sleep. As his kids got older, he would take them to his practices, so

"WHEN IT COMES TIME FOR YOU TO LEAVE, LEAVE A LEGEND."

they could "see the beauty in the process." It was all part of the legacy he was trying to leave. "As parents, you've got to lead by example," he said. "If you want your kids to accomplish whatever they want in life, you have to first show them."

After his playing days ended, he established the Mamba Sports Academy as a place for athletes to compete and learn. "The most important thing you can do is to pay everything you learned forward for the next generation to come," he said. "And that's truly how you create something that lasts forever." As a sports dad, he supported the volleyball interest of his oldest, Natalia, and loved coaching Gianna's

AAU team, the Mambas—teaching the 12-year-olds the intricacies of the triangle offense. As the kids developed their own goals, their dreams became his, including Gianna's ambition to play collegiately at the powerhouse women's basketball program at the University of Connecticut. The two would often travel to UConn home and away games and meet the players.

Sharing his life lessons was a duty he took seriously. He'd sometimes hand out sneakers and write inspiring messages on them, like "Be Legendary" or "Live Mythically." He was trying to bring to life his fantasy for the future: a whole world full of passionate people.

In the last year of Kobe's life, he talked about what he had accomplished and, most importantly, what he had learned. He looked back at that 18-year-old kid who showed up at his first Lakers camp, filled with so much bravado and ambition. "I made a promise to myself," he explained, "that I was going to work hard every single day, so when I retired I would have no regrets."

In the two decades since, he had discovered that there was nothing better on earth than fully committing to something big. That was gold. The other rewards were nice, but fleeting. Every year the NBA would crown another new champion, he explained, and the Oscars would reward a whole new set of movies. That wasn't what mattered. What mattered was the doing.

LESSONS FROM A LEGEND

- 🏀 **STAND UP FOR WHAT'S RIGHT.**
- 🏀 **BUILD A BODY OF WORK TO BE PROUD OF.**
- 🏀 **PAY IT FORWARD. SHARE YOUR INSIGHTS WITH THE NEXT GENERATION.**

MAMBA OUT.

Man! I can't believe how fast 20 years went by. This is crazy. This is absolutely crazy. And you know, to be standing here at center court with you guys, my teammates behind me, and appreciating the journey that we've been on. You know we've been through our ups and been through our downs, and I think the most important part is that we all stayed together throughout.

I grew up a die-hard, I mean a die-hard Laker fan, die-hard. I knew everything about every player that's played here. So to be drafted and then traded to this organization and to spend 20 years here, you can't write something better than this.

I'm more proud not about the championships, but about the down years, because we didn't run. We didn't run. We played through all that stuff and we got our championships and we did it the right way. All I can do here is just thank you guys. Thank you guys for all the years of support. Thank you guys for all the motivation. Thank you for all the inspiration.

What's funny... the thing that had me cracking up all night long was the fact that I go through 20 years of everybody screaming to pass the ball and on the last night they're like, "Don't pass it!" *(big laughs)*

This has been absolutely beautiful. I can't believe it's come to an end. You guys will always be in my heart, and I sincerely, sincerely appreciate it. No words can describe how I feel about you guys. Thank you. Thank you from the bottom of my heart. God, I love you guys. I love you guys.

To my family, my wife, Vanessa, our daughters Nathalia and Gianna, thank you guys for all your sacrifice. For all the hours I spent in the gym working and training, and Vanessa you holding down the family the way that you have, there's no way that I can thank you enough for that. So, from the bottom of my heart, thank you.

What can I say, Mamba out.

—KOBE BRYANT, farewell speech,
Staples Center, Los Angeles, April 14, 2016,
after scoring 60 points in his final game

RESOURCES

MAGAZINES/WEBSITES/ NEWSPAPERS

"The Final Stand"
ESPN Magazine, April 11, 2016

"The Mentors Behind the Mamba"
ESPN Magazine, May 9, 2016

"Life of Reilly: Commuting to Staples Center with Kobe Bryant"
ESPN.com, April 14, 2009

"Pictures of Greatness"
ESPN Kobe Bryant single issue magazine, February 7, 2020

"Kobe Bryant Never Stopped Trying to Inspire."
ESPN Kobe Bryant single issue magazine, February 7, 2020

"Kobe Through the Years"
ESPN Kobe Bryant single issue magazine, February 7, 2020

"Kobe Was Ready to Dominate Hollywood, Too"
ESPN Kobe Bryant single issue magazine, February 7, 2020

"Kobe's Greatness Was Beautiful and Maddening"
ESPN Kobe Bryant single issue magazine, February 7, 2020

"Relentless, Curious and Infinitely Complicated,"
ESPN Kobe Bryant single issue magazine, February 7, 2020

"I'm Glad We Patched Things Up"
ESPN Kobe Bryant single issue magazine, February 7, 2020

"Gigi's Hoop Dreams"
ESPN Kobe Bryant single issue
magazine, February 7, 2020

"What Fueled Kobe's Obsessions"
ESPN Kobe Bryant single issue
magazine, February 7, 2020

"Kobe Bryant Doesn't Want
Your Love"
Esquire, November 2007

"Kobe Bryant Will Always Be
an All-Star of Talking"
GQ, March 2015

"Kobe Goes It Alone"
Newsweek, May 30, 1999

"The End of an Era: A Requiem
for the Kobe-Shaq Feud"
Newsweek, August 27, 2015

"An Oscar Feels Better Than
an NBA Championship"
Newsweek, March 5, 2018

"The Enigma Remains"
Newsweek: Kobe (Special
Commemorative Issue)*, 2020*

"Manchild in the Promised Land"
SLAM, March 1998

"The Road"
SLAM, April 2010

"Leader of the New School"
SLAM, May/June 2019

"Once Upon a Time"
SLAM: Mamba Forever (Special
Collector's Tribute Issue), 2020

"The Conductor"
SLAM: Mamba Forever (Special
Collector's Tribute Issue), 2020

"Inevitable"
SLAM: Mamba Forever (Special
Collector's Tribute Issue), 2020

"Mamba 101"
SLAM: Mamba Forever (Special
Collector's Tribute Issue), 2020

"The Whole Truth"
SLAM: Mamba Forever (Special
Collector's Tribute Issue), 2020

"Renaissance Man 2.0"
SLAM: Mamba Forever (Special
Collector's Tribute Issue), 2020

"Boy II Man"
Sports Illustrated, May 6, 1996

"Show Time!"
Sports Illustrated, April 27, 1998

"Young and Restless"
Sports Illustrated, April 24, 2000

"The End of the Circque de L.A."
Sports Illustrated, July 26, 2004

"81"
Sports Illustrated,
January 30, 2006

"That Killer Instinct"
Sports Illustrated, June 2, 2008

"Alone at Last"
Sports Illustrated, June 22, 2009

"The Final Challenge"
Sports Illustrated, June 7, 2010

"The Last Alpha Dog"
Sports Illustrated, October 21, 2013

"Teachable Moment"
Sports Illustrated,
October 26, 2015

"Local Hero"
SportsIllustrated.com,
December 2, 2015

"The Beautiful Farewell"
Sports Illustrated,
December 7, 2015

"His Moment of Zen"
Sports Illustrated: Kobe Bryant
(Special Retirement Issue), 2016

"Pair of Kings"
Sports Illustrated: Kobe Bryant
(Special Retirement Issue), 2016

"The Next Chapter"
Sports Illustrated, March 7, 2019

"Hoop Dreamer"
Sports Illustrated,
January 28, 2020

"A Competitor Like No Other"
Sports Illustrated: Kobe Bryant
(Special Retirement Issue), 2020

"The Mamba Generation"
Sports Illustrated, Kobe Bryant
(Special Tribute Issue), 2020

"Forever Kobe"
The Undefeated.com,
August 24, 2016

"The Revisionist"
The Washington Post,
November 14, 2018

BOOKS

Kobe Bryant: The Mindset of a Champion, by Steve James

The Mamba Mentality, by Kobe Bryant

Remembering Kobe Bryant, edited by Sean Deveney

INTERVIEWS

"Kobe Bryant Interview/Mamba Mentality," April 25, 2018, USC Performance Science Institute

"Kobe Bryant's Last Great Interview," August 23, 2019, Patrick Bet-David

"Exclusive 1 on 1 with Kobe Bryant in China," October 18, 2019, CloseUp360

"HOPEFULLY I'LL BE REMEMBERED AS A PERSON THAT LEFT NO STONE UNTOUCHED. AND DID EVERYTHING POSSIBLE TO TRY TO REACH HIS FULL POTENTIAL."